1495

LAFITTE THE PIRATE

SOUTHERN LIBRARY SERIES
Published by Pelican Publishing Company

LAFITTE THE PIRATE

CHILDREN OF STRANGERS

OLD LOUISIANA

FABULOUS NEW ORLEANS

END OF AN ERA: NEW ORLEANS, 1850-1860

LOUISIANA HAYRIDE

MARDI GRAS . . . AS IT WAS

GUMBO YA-YA: FOLK TALES OF LOUISIANA

MARDI GRAS: A PICTORIAL HISTORY
OF CARNIVAL IN NEW ORLEANS

NEW ORLEANS AS IT WAS

Lafitte
the Pirate

By
LYLE SAXON

Illustrated by
E. H. Suydam

PELICAN PUBLISHING COMPANY
Gretna 1999

First published by The Century Co. 1930
Published by arrangement with The Century Co.
   by Robert L. Crager & Co. 1950
Published by arrangement with Robert L. Crager & Co.
   by Pelican Publishing Company, Inc. 1989

Pelican paperback edition
First printing, September 1989
Second printing, July 1994
Third printing, December 1999

Library of Congress Cataloging-in-Publication Data

Saxon, Lyle, 1891-1946.
   Lafitte the pirate.

   Reprint. Originally published: New Orleans :
R.L. Crager, 1950.
   Bibliography: p.
   1. Lafitte, Jean. 2. Pirates--Louisiana--Biography.
3. Pirates--Texas--Biography. 4. New Orleans, Battle of,
1815. 5. Privateering--Mexico, Gulf of--History--
19th century. I. Title.
F374.L2S28 1989   973.5'239'092 [B]   89-3899
ISBN 0-88289-395-5

Printed in Canada
Published by Pelican Publishing Company, Inc.
1000 Burmaster Street, Gretna, Louisiana 70053

FOR

MERCEDES GARIG

FOREWORD

NEW ORLEANS, a century ago, produced many fantastic characters, but Jean Lafitte—the pirate who became a famous patriot, then turned back to piracy again—is one of the most extraordinary of them all.

With his brother, Pierre, this young Frenchman came to Louisiana early in the nineteenth century and opened a blacksmith shop. While negro slaves hammered out iron grillwork and lace-like balcony railings at the forge, the brothers took their place in that gay panorama of Creole life, and became well-known figures at the theater, opera, the coffee-houses, the gambling saloons and the quadroon ballrooms.

Secretly, Jean Lafitte was leader of the Baratarians—smugglers who lived among those low-lying islands in the Mexican Gulf, just off the Louisiana coast. Such genius had Lafitte for organization and management that his followers soon numbered more than a thousand men "of every shade of complexion and villany."

Nowadays we would call him a gang-leader or a racketeer; his "racket" was smuggling, then privateer-

Foreword

ing against Spanish slave-ships and, eventually, piracy. He became known to posterity as the last of the great pirates. Claiborne, Louisiana's first American governor, offered a reward for his capture; but the buccaneer swaggered in the streets of New Orleans, a dangerous man whom no one dared molest.

When British vessels approached Louisiana during the War of 1812, the commodore of the invading fleet attempted to enlist the aid of Lafitte and his men against the American forces. Had the pirate accepted, it is probable that the British would have taken New Orleans. Instead, Lafitte pretended to agree, then betrayed the plans of the invading army, and offered the services of himself and his buccaneers to the United States. General Andrew Jackson accepted the offer, and the Baratarians played their part in defeating the British on the plains of Chalmette. Pardoned for all past crimes by President Madison, Lafitte became a popular hero.

But respectability bored him, so he turned again to an outlaw's life. This time he set up his gaudy pirate's kingdom at Galveston Island, on the Texas coast.

Jean Lafitte has been the hero, or villain, of a score of novels: some of the writers have portrayed him as a fearless, guiltless gentleman, a great lover, or a gay deceiver; others have made him a cowardly and bloodthirsty pirate. He has also become a figure in the folklore of America, and hundreds of legendary tales persist. Even to-day, men are digging for the vast treasure

Foreword

which he is said to have buried on the shores of the Gulf of Mexico.

In writing this biography, I have tried to present a truthful picture. It has not been easy. For the greater part, my information is taken from contemporary documents and letters, and from the crumbling files of century-old newspapers. The mass of legendary material is so great, and so disguised as history, that the task of sifting truth from legend has proved a long and difficult one. It was rather like trying to put together a jig-saw puzzle, a portrait of a man which had been cut into a thousand fragments, and further complicated because upon the reverse side of the portrait was another picture similar in coloring; the second picture was that of a mythical pirate.

Just as there are two versions of nearly every story concerning the buccaneer, there is a controversy even as to the spelling of his name: in the earlier letters, his signature appears as "Lafitte," or "La Fite," while in those letters written after 1815, he spells his name "Laffite." I have chosen the more familiar form.

Many have assisted me in research work, and I wish to acknowledge my debt, and to thank the following: Frank C. Patten, chief librarian, and Miss Octavia F. Rogan and Miss Hazel A. Millard, all of the Rosenberg Library at Galveston, Texas; Miss Essae M. Culver, director of the Louisiana Library Commission at Baton Rouge; Miss Carrie Freret, librarian for the Louisiana

Foreword

Historical Society at the Cabildo, New Orleans; Henry Lanause, keeper of records at the New Orleans Board of Health; the archivist at the Saint Louis Cathedral, New Orleans; Mrs. Cammie G. Henry, of Melrose Plantation, for the use of her library; Dr. Theodore Engelbach of Grande Isle; and to those others, whose letters and documents are listed in the bibliography at the end of this volume.

E. H. Suydam went with me to New Orleans, and out among the islands and bayous of Barataria, in order to make sketches in the haunts of the buccaneers. His illustrations form an important part of the record.

L. S.

CONTENTS

xi

Contents

ILLUSTRATIONS

ILLUSTRATIONS

Chapter I

THE BROTHERS LAFITTE

"DEAR BROTHER NED, I have seen the notorious Captain Lafitte . . ."

The quill sputtered in the hand of the excited boy, and young Esau Glasscock let fall a large blot of ink upon the letter which he was writing to his brother in Virginia. He stopped to repair the damage as best he could; he sprinkled sand heavily upon the sodden paper, and then continued with more calmness: "And our father has bought six likely negroes from the barracoon at Grande Terre."

In late November, 1809, a plantation owner by the name of Glasscock went to New Orleans for the purpose of buying slaves. He took his eighteen-year-old son, Esau, with him. The boy had never visited the city before and he found it altogether extraordinary. Accordingly, upon his return to the plantation, which lay along the Mississippi River somewhere between Baton Rouge and Natchez, Esau wrote a full account of his visit to his brother Ned who was at boarding-school. It is from this faded and torn letter that we get our first real picture of Lafitte—the man whose name was the terror of the Mexican Gulf a century ago.

But perhaps it will be better to take up the boy's letter in its logical order.

The Glasscocks, father and son, had a difficult passage down the river to New Orleans. The weather was cold and their negro oarsmen were unfamiliar with the treacherous currents of the Mississippi. Once their boat was nearly upset in a whirlpool. One night they were forced to camp on the river bank, but not without uneasiness, for river-pirates made frequent assaults upon travelers. The second night they spent in the hospitable home of a Creole planter, where they were entertained "as though we had been relatives instead of strangers."

The levee at New Orleans was astir when they arrived. Many flatboats were unloading, and the red-shirted flatboatmen shouted and cursed. Negroes sang as they rolled the cotton bales. There were Indians "pretty nearly naked" at the public market which stood behind the levee, and the streets were crowded with "men of every nation under the sun." The Glasscocks sought sup-

4

The Brothers Lafitte

per and a lodging for the night. They were well fed and well provided for, but Esau found the guests at the hostelry "somewhat uncouth and savage" in appearance; and he was kept awake half the night by roistering in the street and in the courtyard of the inn.

Next morning they went to call upon Governor Claiborne, a fellow Virginian with whom the elder Glasscock had some slight acquaintance; but the governor kept them cooling their heels for an hour, and when they saw him at last they found him friendly but "near distracted with anxiety which some public affairs had given him." The call was not altogether satisfactory but, as they were leaving the governor, Mr. Glasscock had the great good fortune to meet his young friend Mr. Grymes, who "carried us off to his residence, despite our father's protestations," where the Glasscocks, *père et fils,* remained for the duration of their visit.

This turn of affairs pleased Esau, for John Randolph Grymes was indeed a jolly young gentleman. Like Governor Claiborne, he was a Virginian by birth, and a lawyer. Only the year before he had completed his studies and had been admitted to the bar in Virginia. Shortly after, he had come to Louisiana in search of money and adventure. In the autumn of 1809 when Esau met him, he was only twenty-four years old, but he had already made a place for himself as an American lawyer in Creole New Orleans.

When Grymes and the Glasscocks left the governor's

office, they "repaired immediately to a coffee-house" for refreshment and conversation, and it was at this juncture that the elder Glasscock told Grymes the reason for his visit to the city. An auction of slaves had been advertised in Le Courier de la Louisiane, and it was Glasscock's intention to attend the auction and buy half a dozen laborers for his plantation.

But Grymes assured him that there was to be no auction; some legal tangle had ensnarled the slave-dealer and his wares, and the sale had been postponed—perhaps for a long time. There was a scarcity of slaves for sale in New Orleans, and the supply was far insufficient to the demand, since the embargo placed upon the importation of Africans by the United States. However—and here Mr. Grymes lowered his voice—there were other means of acquiring negroes. And he mentioned the name of Lafitte.

Immediately the father began to ask questions, for the name was familiar to him, and the exploits of the smugglers of Barataria were common gossip. But was it true, he asked, that the brothers Lafitte were outlaws?

Mr. Grymes shrugged his shoulders—a trick that this adaptable young man had learned already from the Creoles—and laughed. No, he did not think so. The Lafitte brothers owned a blacksmith's shop on Saint Philip Street and Mr. Glasscock could go there and judge for himself. It was true that the Lafittes had many slaves for sale, but they were merely representatives for others,

The Brothers Lafitte

those *contrebandiers* who procured negroes mysteriously out of nowhere. Perhaps, said Mr. Grymes, it is not good to inquire too closely into things which do not concern you, and if the Lafittes could supply the slaves you needed, why not buy them? He added that the Lafittes' negroes were cheaper than those advertised on the public market.

The upshot of the matter was that the elder of the Glasscocks went to the Lafitte forge, and after some conversation, determined to accompany Jean Lafitte, the younger of the brothers, to the slave warehouse at Grande Terre, some sixty miles away. He departed at sunrise the next morning, leaving young Esau to the tender mercies of the jolly Mr. Grymes.

Left to his own devices, Esau took a walk about the city. Everything was new and strange to him. In his boyhood in Virginia and his early young manhood on a Louisiana plantation he had heard much talk of New Orleans, but the city that he saw on his walk that day proved disappointing.

The streets were crowded with men of many nations, French, Spanish, Italian; negro slaves shuffled by, bearing bales and baskets on their heads. Through open doorways he caught glimpses of merchants arranging their wares, and he was impressed by the "richness and extravagance" of some of the silks, laces and madras which he observed piled high upon shelves in the stores. Everywhere there were "free people of color," those refugees

Lafitte the Pirate

from Santo Domingo who were then flocking to New Orleans to escape the massacres in the West Indian islands. The houses of the city he found "of foreign appearance" with walled gardens and tight-barred windows; only the Church of Saint Louis and the Principal (or court-house) pleased him. The streets were muddy and the walking difficult; a stench rose from the ditches which stood level-full of water. Once, in crossing a ditch he slipped and nearly fell; he heard laughter, and turning, saw two dark-haired girls looking down from behind a half-open window blind. He smiled back at them, "whereupon the elder girl let fall a red rose, and laughed again and clapped shut the window."

And so the days passed. At night he sat long with Mr. Grymes over the wine bottles, or went with him on a visit to this one or that. But on the fourth day of his father's absence, Esau became worried. All the protestations of his host did not allay his fears. Those swamps and bayous between New Orleans and the Gulf of Mexico had swallowed up more than one traveler, and Esau was fearful that his father had met with accident, or worse. So in the late afternoon he went to the Lafitte forge in Saint Philip Street, seeking news.

A giant negro at the smithy directed him to a knocker on the courtyard gate, and he was admitted presently to an inclosed garden where oleanders and date-palms grew. In one of the rooms which opened upon this courtyard, a man, a woman and a small boy were at supper. The man

8

THE COTTAGE OF THE BROTHERS LAFITTE

THIAC'S BLACKSMITH SHOP

came outside, wiping his mouth on a napkin. It was Pierre Lafitte, the older of the brothers.

"He is a strapping man of middle size," Esau wrote to his brother, "with light hair growing low on his forehead. His eyes are dark and his teeth very white. He speaks English with a strong accent of French. He assured me of our father's safety, saying that the trip was arduous and difficult, and that unfavorable winds and tides sometimes delayed the boats, etc."

In the course of the conversation, Esau's fears were stilled, and presently "at the insistence of the gentleman" he found himself seated at supper with the family, and drinking sweet wine from a silver mug. The woman was swarthy and dark, and Pierre Lafitte said that she spoke no English as she had lately come from Santo Domingo. The little boy, who was exceedingly like his father, was called Pierre. And he was not the son of the woman who served the wine. "He is," wrote Esau, "the son of this Mr. Lafitte by a previous marriage."

Mellow with wine, he returned to Mr. Grymes after nightfall, no longer fearful for his father's safe return. And so it turned out, for in due time Mr. Glasscock came back with the "six likely negroes" which Esau mentioned at the beginning of his letter.

The Glasscocks planned to leave the following day for the plantation, but the merry Mr. Grymes persuaded them to remain another day in order to attend a ball on Sunday night.

Lafitte the Pirate

The elder Glasscock made some slight objection (possibly on moral grounds, being a Virginia gentleman) but
they were easily overridden by his host and his son. Accordingly "two hours after supper" on Sunday, the three
went to the ball-room, which was also on Saint Philip
Street not far away from the levee.

Esau, discreet youth, gives but a meager mention of
the ball itself, except to say that "the quadroon women
are as beautiful as possible" and that they are excellent
dancers. But this is enough, for the quadroon balls have
been described in all of their florid detail by other visitors
to New Orleans at the period, and we shall speak of them
again later. Suffice to say that Esau and his father, accompanied by the faithful Grymes, peeped that night
beneath the crust of society and saw there a fascinating
revel. The golden-colored girls, dressed in fine laces and
damasks, wore sparkling jewels, and appeared like
women from "some foreign country"; while along the
wall, impassive, with slowly waving fans, sat their turbaned mothers, women of strange dignity, some still
carrying traces of ravaged beauty. Soft-footed negroes
moved about carrying silver trays of cordials. Violins
throbbed and guitars tinkled. And the beaux and the dandies of New Orleans moved through the crowd, their
ruffled shirt bosoms white against their tight-fitting suits
of dark broadcloth. Candle-light shone on golden shoulders and quivering plumes. Fans fluttered and dark eyes
flashed.

The Brothers Lafitte

But it was in the gaming-room adjoining the ball-room that Esau saw the Lafittes. Pierre, he recognized at once, and his father introduced him to the younger brother. Esau fell under the spell of his personality at once. "He is tall, with pale skin, and he has large dark eyes. He is clean-shaven except for a beard extending part-way down his cheeks." He rose from the card-table to shake hands with Grymes and the boy. "He greeted our father as an old friend, as they had spent some days together in the boats." There was a brief conversation, and Jean Lafitte returned to his game of cards, with "half-a-dozen gentlemen who were somewhat under the influence of wine." Later in the evening Esau saw Jean Lafitte again "this time in company with a quadroon woman, hardly more than a child, with liquid black eyes, such as many of them possess, but somewhat too thin for my taste." They were drinking cordial together beside a window. Esau comments that Jean Lafitte has exceedingly narrow feet, elegantly shod.

It is a pleasant picture that the boy gives us, and it is good to see the brothers Lafitte in a moment of happiness. In 1809, when he saw them, they were both young men—Jean Lafitte was twenty-nine years old, and Pierre a few years older—and they had not yet become entirely entangled in the web of duplicity and crime which was to make them outcasts and hunted men a few years afterward.

Chapter II

AT THE BLACKSMITH SHOP

JEAN and Pierre Lafitte owned and operated a black-smith shop in Saint Philip Street, New Orleans. As early as 1809—as we have seen from Esau's letter—they had formed connections with the smugglers of Barataria, that beautiful and mysterious country which is neither land nor water and which stretches away from the city to the Mexican Gulf, west of the mouth of the Mississippi. For half a century the marshlands of Barataria had been the hiding place for smugglers.

Life was simple in those early days of the nineteenth century in New Orleans, and the Lafittes, although well supplied with worldly goods, lived in an unpretentious cottage near their forge. Their dwelling was at the corner of Saint Philip and Bourbon streets, a few short squares from the court-house and the Church of Saint Louis. The cottage stood flush with the sidewalk and adjoined a garden which was screened from the street by a high wall.

At the Blacksmith Shop

With them lived Adelaide Maselari, a dark and handsome woman from Santo Domingo. She was Pierre Lafitte's mistress and not his wife, as Esau had supposed.
The elder Lafitte had brought her with him from the
West Indian islands. She is, at best, a shadowy figure,
moving about the cottage and courtyard, filling the wine-
glasses; and were it not for certain records in the
archives of the Church of Saint Louis one might doubt
her reality altogether.

A miniature of Pierre Lafitte, evidently painted in his
young manhood, and probably painted in France, shows
him as a full-blooded young gentleman in a bottle-green
coat and lace frills. He has large, dark eyes with a thread
of white showing beneath the pupil; his hair is light
brown and grows low on his forehead; he wears it parted
in the middle and drawn back over his ears. His lips are
full and red, and one would say that the young man was
fond of the good things of life, and that he enjoyed both
wine and women. But perhaps this is going too far, and
one must not conjecture as to his early exploits of which
we know nothing; but certain it is that lust and liquor
played their part in his later life. This miniature was
probably painted twelve years or more before we had our
first glimpse of him, as he walked into the courtyard
among the oleanders, wiping his mouth on a napkin.

It is unfortunate that there is no authentic portrait of
Jean Lafitte aside from the small picture which hangs in
the Cabildo in New Orleans. This painting by the artist

Lafitte the Pirate

Jarvis is said to depict Jean and Pierre Lafitte and Dominique You, the associate of the Lafittes. The three men are pictured at night, as they sit drinking by the firelight. It was painted in 1812, and as Jarvis knew the Lafittes, it may be that the sketch is a faithful likeness. But the figures are so small, and their attitudes are such that one gets but an imperfect impression of Jean Lafitte. True, he is tall and dark—that much is certain—but he is shown singing, and his open mouth distorts his face. Pierre Lafitte, the standing figure in the composition, is somewhat stout, and Dominique You is a typical pirate, swarthy and menacing. There has been some argument as to the authenticity of the portraits, but if one considers the life of John Wesley Jarvis it does not seem unlikely that he held drinking bouts with the smugglers.

Jarvis was a nephew of John Wesley, founder of Methodism, and though he inherited the name of his renowned relative, he was occasionally given to unmethodistic conduct. He spent some time in New Orleans, entertaining much and being entertained, and starting a round of witticisms that were the talk of the day. It is also said that his convivial habits led to the deterioration of his work and his ultimate poverty. At any rate, he painted a picture of the Lafittes, and this imperfect sketch of Jean is the only picture that exists, aside from rough drawings made from memory. If he sat for a portrait, as his brother did, the likeness has disappeared.

All of the contemporary accounts agree that Jean

14

At the Blacksmith Shop

Lafitte was a handsome man. He stood six feet tall, and he was slim and well made. And he was extraordinarily strong. He was known as an expert with the foils, and it was rumored that he had killed a man in a duel in Charleston—an affair of honor in which a mysterious woman played a part. Perhaps there may be some truth in the story, for certain it is that Jean Lafitte was attractive to women. His hair was sleek and black and his profile was classic in its regularity. He smiled seldom, but when he did it was with sparkling black eyes and a sudden flash of white teeth. Usually he went clean-shaven, but sometimes he allowed his beard to grow black along his cheeks and affected sideburns. His grace of manner and his quick wit are recalled by many writers, and it is certain that he was a man of great personal charm. Men and women alike fell under his spell, and it is probable that more than one closely guarded Creole maiden sighed in vain as he passed her window.

For the Lafittes occupied a peculiar position in New Orleans. They were accepted socially by the men, in much the same fashion that the fencing-masters were accepted, but the Lafittes were not asked to meet the wives and daughters of their business acquaintances. The only time that the brothers are known to have appeared at a ball where women of the best families gathered, was the festival in honor of Andrew Jackson shortly after the battle of New Orleans in 1815. Their presence there is well established, as we shall see in another chapter; but in 1809 we only know that the Lafittes attended the Quadroon Balls, and we find their names affixed to various lists as "donors" for public functions, both at the theater and the opera. They were also patrons and backers for Mr. Turpin who conducted the Hôtel de la Marine and a cabaret besides.

Very little was known of the early life of the Lafittes except that they were Frenchmen who had come to Louisiana by way of the West Indian islands. They were known to be agents for the smugglers of Barataria, and they dealt in slaves as well as in merchandise. In 1809, the warehouse at the forge proving insufficient, they had opened a shop on Royal Street, where they displayed linens and silks and other imported goods. From the scope of their activities it appears that they had been in New Orleans for several years before our first sight of them. and it is probable that they had visited New Orleans, at least, as early as 1804.

It is not on record that any one inquired into the past of the Lafittes at this time. The questions were to come later, and the answers were to set historians guessing in another age. But as we first see the brothers, they are living simply in their cottage, and keeping close watch on their business interests. They had a small circle of intimates.

Their friends would gather in the courtyard in the late afternoon. Jean Lafitte stretched his long and well-muscled legs in a red hammock, and reclined, apparently

At the Blacksmith Shop

half asleep, only to rouse suddenly with flashing eyes
when some one made a statement with which he did not
agree. He had the droll habit of closing his left eye as he
talked. It was almost a wink, and sometimes it proved dis-
concerting to those whom he addressed: one wondered if
his earnest words, usually sprinkled plentifully with fine
phrases, had the ring of sincerity, or whether his half-
closed eye held some secret significance.

A strangely assorted group gathered there in the
courtyard under the oleander-trees—men from various
walks of life. There was the suave Sauvinet, a well-to-do
man who lived near-by, a capitalist and *rentier,* whose
money (or so it was said) went into the illegal traffickings
of the Lafittes. There was Laporte, small, dark, silent,
smiling, who kept the accounts of the business; there was
Huette, a planter of Bayou Saint John, whose city residence was near the Sauvinets'; and there was "old Thiac"
the blacksmith—a real blacksmith this time—a brawny
fellow whose forge was near the levee. Thiac had a bad
reputation with the authorities. He had been arrested for
receiving stolen goods, and again for harboring stolen
slaves at his smithy. . . . And always, moving softly
about among the men, the dark Santo Domingan woman,
Adelaide Maselari, and the little son of Pierre.

It is probable that, when the affairs of business were
settled, that the conversation in the courtyard turned to
the affairs of Europe. News traveled slowly in those days,
and men of New Orleans read the pages of Le Courier

Lafitte the Pirate

de la Louisiane with feverish interest. In 1809 the pages of this newspaper carried the accounts of Napoleon's invasion of Spain. To-day we can turn the yellowed pages and read for ourselves the news of the Peninsular Wars, and of how in 1808 Napoleon had made his brother Joseph king of Portugal, and had transferred the throne of Naples, which Joseph had been occupying, to his brother-in-law Murat, thus giving away thrones and kingdoms with prodigal hands. But Portugal rose in wrath. The people from the Pyrenees to the Strait of Gibraltar were flying to arms. Sir Arthur Wellesley, afterwards Duke of Wellington, was sent with a force from England to aid Spain. Joseph fled from his throne, and Napoleon found it necessary to take to the field himself. He entered the Peninsula at the head of eighty thousand men, and routing the Spaniards wherever he met them, entered Madrid in triumph and reseated Joseph on the Spanish throne. . . . In 1809 Napoleon was at war in Austria and was marching on Vienna. Francis the First was done for. . . . It was in 1809 that the Pope excommunicated Napoleon, but Napoleon had him arrested and dragged across the Alps and held in captivity for four years, and the Papal States and Holland were joined to the French Empire. . . .

But the news in the paper was faulty enough, and much was printed on hearsay; it was not until two years later that the people of New Orleans were to read a detailed account of Napoleon's invasion of Spain in the first

At the Blacksmith Shop

issues of Niles' Weekly Register, a Baltimore paper which was popular with the English-speaking people of Louisiana.

As a boy of fourteen, Jean Lafitte had witnessed the Reign of Terror in France, and Pierre Lafitte, it was said, had served for a time in the French Navy. And although Louisiana was now their adopted country, they followed Napoleon's career with the keenest interest. Sauvinet, their friend, had interests in France and relatives there, and old Thiac the blacksmith was always interested in the news of a fight; so conversation in the courtyard must have been lively enough as the men took their ease there at twilight, and the dark Adelaide moved about filling the glasses.

Chapter III

OLD NEW ORLEANS

THE first quarter of the nineteenth century was a fantastic period in Louisiana, and the Lafittes were characteristic of the time in which they lived. In order to understand their strange careers it is necessary to know something of that tatterdemalion among cities, New Orleans.

Founded in 1718 by the French, it continued for fifty years a provincial French town set down in the lush wilderness near the mouth of the Mississippi River. A never-ending pageant of sailing ships had crossed and recrossed the Atlantic and had come through the Mexican Gulf from France to the Louisiana coast. Slowly the ships came, but come they did, disgorging a strange crew: soldiers, aristocrats, adventurers, outcasts, criminals from

Old New Orleans

the Paris jails, nuns, priests, pirates, smugglers, and solid men and women from the middle class who had come, like all the others, to make a fortune in the New World.

The history of the town had been tempestuous: there had been bloody wars with Indians, and battles against fire, flood and famine. Tropical hurricanes, blowing up from the Caribbean Sea, had brought death and destruction to the growing community. The Mississippi had overflowed its banks, had broken through the inadequate levees and inundated the streets. Epidemics materially reduced the population. Still a steady stream of settlers poured in. Thrifty Germans came by the shipload and settled in the fertile lands along the river bank adjoining the city. Slowly, slowly a network of plantations spread further and further into the wilderness; and slowly the city grew.

In 1769 Louisiana had come under the domination of Spain. The people of New Orleans had been bitterly resentful at first, and there had been bloodshed. But the rule of Spain proved mild enough, and, with the intermarriage of Spanish officers and French colonial girls, the population blended into Creolism—neither French nor Spanish, but a combination of both—a combination further softened by the semitropical climate of Louisiana. In 1803, when the United States took possession, New Orleans was nearly a century old, a sophisticated and civilized community—and it was as unlike the American cities of the Atlantic seaboard as though it had been on another continent.

The first American Territorial Governor was W. C. C. Claiborne, a young but benevolent gentleman from Virginia, and to his sad lot fell the task of trying to bring about harmony between the Creoles and the Americans who were coming to settle in the city. One has only to look into Claiborne's official letter books to see his dilemma. On January 10, 1804, we find him writing to James Madison as follows:

"The credulity of the people is only equalled by their ignorance; and a virtuous magistrate, resting entirely for support on the suffrages and good will of his fellow citizens in this quarter, would at any time be exposed to immediate ruin by the machinations of a few base individuals, who with some exertion and address might make the people think and act against their interests." And in another letter he wrote: "The population is composed of so heterogeneous a mass, such prejudices exist, and there are so many different interests to reconcile, that I fear no administration or form of government can give general satisfaction."

Nevertheless, he did the best he could, and it is doubtful if any one could have done better.

New Orleans had been under the rule of Spain for thirty-four years prior to 1803. Immigrants from Nova Scotia, from the Canary Islands and from Málaga had passed through the city into the rural districts. Thousands

Old New Orleans

of "brute negroes" had been brought in aboard the slave-ships and had been sold in New Orleans, and nearly every dwelling had slave-quarters in the courtyard.

Claiborne was right when he called it a "heterogeneous mass," for that is exactly what it was. And everywhere the restless American was conspicuous; and he seemed to survey the city with an air of ownership which was bitter to the Creole's heart.

The city was fast becoming one of the chief seaports of America. In 1803 the tonnage in the harbor increased more than thirty-seven per cent. It exported, of the products of the province alone, a value of more than two million dollars. Its imports reached $2,500,000. Thirty-four thousand bales of cotton; 4,500 hogsheads of sugar; 2,000 barrels of molasses; rice, peltries, indigo, lumber, to the value of $500,000; 50,000 barrels of flour; 3,000 barrels of beef and pork; 2,000 thousands of tobacco; and goodly quantities of corn, butter, hams, meal, lard, beans, hides, staves and cordage passed that year across the levee.

Heretofore all of this business had been transacted by the Creoles, but now new American firms were opening almost every day. The names above the offices were the same names that appeared on the sign-boards of New York and Philadelphia. The very year of the Louisiana Purchase the Creole began to fear his American competitor.

In March 1804 Congress passed an act, dividing the

Lafitte the Pirate

province into two parts on the present northern boundary
of Louisiana, giving each a distinct government, and to
the lower the title of "The Territory of Orleans." The
act, which took effect the following October, interdicted
the slave trade. Promptly anger broke forth. The whole

economic system of Louisiana was built up on slave labor,
the Creoles argued, and slaves must be had at any cost.
. . . There was talk of a Spanish recession.

The fear of Spain was very real, and when Aaron
Burr appeared in New Orleans in June 1805, Claiborne
was almost at his wits' end. But the Burr conspiracy for

SPANISH CUSTOM HOUSE ON BAYOU ST. JOHN

THE FRENCH MARKET, NEAR THE LEVEE

the formation of a Western Empire in the United States came to nothing, and after his arrest the American authorities in New Orleans were easier in mind. But Spaniards in adjoining territories continued to harass those in the Territory of Orleans.

Since the cession of Louisiana to the United States, the inhabitants of those parts of the Territory which bordered on Spanish possessions had suffered from the loss of their slaves. The negroes ran away and sought the protection of a foreign flag, under which they were induced to believe that their condition would be improved. Each year Claiborne and the Spanish Governors had much correspondence on this matter, but the condition grew steadily worse.

A letter from Dr. Sibley of Natchitoches to Governor Claiborne gives an interesting sidelight on Spanish methods:

"Nothing important has occurred here lately since the desertion of about thirty negroes," he writes on December 14, 1808. "Things cannot long remain as they are; it would be better, the people say, for them to be under the Government of Spain than thus situated. How long their allegiance to our Government will remain without protection, I know not. The negroes were furnished with Spanish cockades at Nacadoches, a dance given them, and since they have been marched off to the Trinity River, singing 'Long live Ferdinand the Seventh.' "

By 1809 the embargo against the importation of

slaves caused a shortage of negroes throughout the territory. Prices rose. There were few slaves to be had and there was an ever-increasing demand.

The Lafittes saw their chance—and took it.

Chapter IV

THE SMUGGLERS

"European wars in the closing years of the Eighteenth Century developed a class of men who had become expert in the practice of privateering," says Fortier in his "History of Louisiana." "And in the early years of the Nineteenth Century, privateers claiming to operate under French 'letters of marque' infested the Gulf of Mexico. Spain's commerce was the object of their prey."

These sea-rovers had their headquarters at Guadaloupe and Martinique, but the islands were captured by the British in 1806, and in 1810 the privateers were driven out. They then transferred the base of their operations to Barataria Bay on the southern coast of Louisiana. At about the same time that they made their appearance in

Lafitte the Pirate

the territory adjacent to New Orleans, the province of Colombia declared itself independent of Spanish rule, and the government of the seaport of Carthagena granted letters of marque to the privateers. These adaptable seafaring gentlemen lost no time in hauling down the flag of France and hoisting the standard of the new republic.

The islands on the Louisiana coast to which they now brought their prizes had been inhabited for more than fifty years by fishermen and trappers. These settlers had soon found that smuggling was more profitable, and during the Spanish domination of New Orleans had built up a fairly well organized system for slipping merchandise past the Spanish custom-house at New Orleans. Various well-to-do merchants bought from them their supplies, and the practice of smuggling was not frowned upon by the citizens of the city.

Grace King, the historian, writes:

Smuggling, as well as privateering, had always been a regular branch of the commerce of Louisiana. In the old French colonial days the uncertainty of supplies from the mother-country had rendered it almost a necessity of existence: under the ironclad tariff policy of Spain it was quite a necessity. By the time of the cession of the Territory to the United States, smuggling prices and smuggling relations had been so long established in the community that they had become a part of the habits of life there. The prices of smuggled goods were far cheaper than they could possibly have been if the customs duties had been levied upon them, and the relations with the purveyors of cheap goods were, what they will always be be-

The Smugglers

tween consumers and purveyors of cheap goods, confidential and intimate; and there was in addition a general feeling that a laudable principle of conservatism and independence, rather than otherwise, was shown in ignoring the American pretensions of moral superiority over the old standard.

In the letters of Governor Claiborne we get his reaction to this attitude on the part of the Creoles. We find him writing to President Madison in January, 1810:

It is confidently reported that two or three vessels have lately sailed from Pensacola for the Coast of Africa, and design to return with a cargo of negroes. These will be carried to the rich settlement of Baton Rouge, and such as cannot be sold there will probably be conveyed across the Mississippi and disposed of in the Territory of Orleans.

Claiborne had been correctly informed, for on September 6th of the same year we find Thomas Bolling Robertson, Secretary of the Territory, writing to Madison:

You have no doubt heard of the late introduction of African slaves among us. Two cargoes have been already smuggled into this Territory by way of Barataria and Bayou Lafourche, and I am fully convinced from a variety of circumstances which have come to my knowledge, that an extensive and well-laid plan exists to evade and defeat the operation of the laws on the subject. The open and daring course which is now pursued by a set of brigands who infest our coast, and overrun our country, is calculated to excite the strongest indignation in the breast of every man who feels the slightest respect for the wise and politic institutions under which we live. At this moment, upwards of one hundred slaves are held by some of our own citizens in the very teeth of the most positive laws, and notwithstanding every exertion which has been made, so general seems to be the disposition to aid in the concealment, that but faint hopes are entertained of detecting the parties and bringing them to punishment.

This old letter has a strangely modern flavor. If one could substitute the word "liquor" for the word "slaves" it would be easy enough to understand the attitude of the Creoles. The prohibition of African slaves in New Orleans proved as unpopular as the prohibition of liquor, a century later. And as the prohibition laws produced a horde of illicit traders in alcohol, so this prohibitive act against the introduction of slaves brought the smugglers of Barataria into immediate notoriety as freebooters of negroes.

Until the year 1810, Jean and Pierre Lafitte had acted only as the city-representatives for the smugglers. Their forge in Saint Philip Street and their shop in Royal Street had taken care of their quota of contraband negroes as well as quantities of illicitly secured merchandise. Their relations with the smugglers made it necessary for them to travel back and forth between the islands that fringed the Mexican Gulf, and the city. And these trips increased in frequency in the summer of 1810, for there was trouble among the smuggling gentry.

The Smugglers

The native inhabitants of the islands, those somewhat lackadaisical fishermen and *contrebandiers,* were brought into competition with the newly arrived privateers from Martinique and Guadaloupe. The population of Grande Isle and Grande Terre, those adjoining islands at the seaward side of Barataria Bay, doubled itself in 1810. The privateers and smugglers formed two distinct groups, and they were soon warring upon each other. The struggle was not unlike a modern clash between rival gangs of racketeers.

A vessel belonging to the native smugglers was returning from a voyage to the African coast. Somewhere in the Mexican Gulf it was attacked by privateers—or pirates, if you prefer to call them so—and the cargo was stolen. The smugglers' slave-ship was never seen again, but the negroes turned up at the barracoon at Grande Terre. In some way the story leaked out, and immediately a blood vendetta began. From the meager accounts which have come down to us, it would appear that there was much bloodshed on the islands in the summer months of that year, but by October a truce had been declared. It was generally agreed that some sort of government was necessary, some code which could be enforced.

A delegation representing both parties called upon the Lafittes, and it was at this time—sometime during the month of October, 1810—that Jean Lafitte made the decision which was to color his entire life thereafter. He became a privateer.

31

Lafitte the Pirate

A vessel was fitted out at his own expense and he sailed to Carthagena. He returned with letters of marque, and—or so tradition tells us—with a Spanish prize to boot. Before the end of the year he was one of the leaders in the strange republic of pirates and *contrebandiers* now gathered at Barataria. It is not surprising that he soon assumed leadership among them, for he was a man of keen intelligence and quick wit. He was strong physically, and he had money. Also, he had friends in New Orleans among the moneyed merchants, and he could dispose of the goods which the ships brought in—no matter how strange the prizes might be.

Pierre Lafitte would have been the logical choice for a leader among the Baratarians, but in 1810 he was ill. Sometime during the summer he suffered "a stroke" (probably of apoplexy) which had left one side of his face paralyzed. It is true that he recovered and before many months was as strong as before, but forever after he was incapable of controlling the muscles of his left eye. In subsequent accounts, he is described as "somewhat cross-eyed."

It was in October, as we have seen, that Jean Lafitte cast his lot with the Baratarians and became, literally, one of them; and in the same month another event of importance occurred in the house on Saint Philip Street. In the Baptismal Records of the Church of Saint Louis (now the Saint Louis Cathedral), register VI, folio 117, number 486, we find that Marie Josephe Lafitte was born on

The Smugglers

October 27th, 1810, and was baptised January 16, 1811, "illegitimate daughter of Pierre Lafitte, a native of Bayonne in France, and of Adelaide Maselari, a native of San Domingo."

Chapter V

BARATARIA

In the spring of 1811, Jean Lafitte built a house for himself near the slave warehouse on Grande Terre. The dwelling was erected on a slight elevation facing the sea, and was constructed of brick coated outside with a mixture of pulverized oyster-shells and plaster. It was a sturdy, low house with iron-barred windows and a wide veranda looking out toward the Gulf. And upon this veranda Lafitte lounged in the late afternoon, lying in a red hammock in much the same fashion that he had lounged in the courtyard in New Orleans.

Men living to-day at the neighboring settlement on Grande Isle can tell you stories of Lafitte and his house—stories that they heard from their grandfathers and

34

grandmothers. For these men are the descendents of Lafitte's corsairs. It is an odd thing, but the tales are all pictorial. They give glimpses of the man, but only vivid
fragments.

Take this, for example, told to me by Benio Rigaud,
who said that his grandmother had told him the story,
over and over:

It was night and the little girl had been asleep for a
long time when her father awakened her. He was laughing and a little drunk. . . . "A man must drink a little,
you know, for his pleasure; it's nature." He told her to get
dressed, that he wanted to take her over to Lafitte's house
on Grande Terre. The privateers were gambling, and
some dispute had arisen. All the money on the table was to
go to one man, but a disinterested person was needed to
"cut the cards." Rigaud, who had been an onlooker at the
game, volunteered to bring his little Marie, and he had
come over in his boat to get her.

Marie's mother was frightened. Suppose those
drunken gamblers began to fight and killed her baby . . .
what then? But Rigaud was firm; he had given his word
and he intended to keep it. Accordingly, the mother,
"weeping like a fountain," dressed Marie, and the father
carried her down to his boat. It was dark and the child
was afraid and cried. Her father lost patience with her.
What nonsense! Mr. Lafitte was a fine gentleman and his
friends were like him, good fellows.

Rigaud beached his boat on Grande Terre and led the

Lafitte the Pirate

little girl across the sand and through the veranda into the big house. Candles were burning, and there were many men gathered around a table. Mr. Lafitte, "a tall gentleman dressed in black," was standing up with a pistol in his hand. The men had been drinking, and there were silver dishes lying on the floor. One of the men had gold earrings in his ears. The little girl, "trembling like a leaf," went up to the table and the cards were given her. She drew one from the deck and turned it face up. It was the ten of diamonds. Lafitte laughed and raked up all the gold coins that were lying scattered there. The man with the earrings cursed and went out of the door, and the other men jeered as he went. Lafitte gave the little girl a big gold coin. It was a Spanish piece worth twenty dollars. Marie held it tight in her hand all the way home.

"And if I've heard my grandmother tell that story once, I've heard her tell it fifty times," said Rigaud, as he sat there on the beach at Grande Isle, "and she never changed a word of it."

There has been much discussion among historians concerning the name Barataria, that haunt of pirates and smugglers. "It will be remembered," writes Grace King, "that Barataria was the name of the island presented by the frolicsome duchess to Sancho Panza, for his sins, as he learned to consider it. How or when the name came to Louisiana is still to be discovered, whether directly from 'Don Quixote,' or from the source which supplied Le-

Barataria

Sage with it, the etymology of the word—*barateur,* mean-ing cheap, *barato,* cheap things."

Webster's dictionary offers another suggestion in the definition of the word "barratry." The French word is *barraterie,* and the Provençal equivalent is *barataria,* and there are two definitions: first, "The practice of exciting and encouraging lawsuits and quarrels," and, second, "A fraudulent breach of duty or willful act of known illegal-ity on the part of a master of a ship, in his character of master, or of the mariners, to the injury of the owner of the ship or cargo, and without his consent. It includes every breach of trust committed with dishonest purpose, as by running away with the ship, sinking her or desert-ing her, etc., or by embezzling the cargo."

To designate a locality by such a name as Barataria is to give it a dubious reputation from the start; but we cannot blame Jean Lafitte for that, for old maps, made before Lafitte's day, carry the word.

That section of Louisiana which bears the name, and which stretches out from the banks of the Mississippi sixty miles or more, southward to the Gulf, is like the rest of the coast of Louisiana, a sea-marsh. It is a vast, wet, level plain, covered everywhere with rustling marsh-grasses higher than a man's head. In traveling by boat from New Orleans toward the Gulf, one is never quite sure where the land ends and the water begins, for the whole "trembling prairie" as it is called, is crossed and recrossed with hundreds of placid bayous, still waters

Lafitte the Pirate

which reflect the high-piled clouds. These lagoons lie in serpentine coils, turning back upon themselves; many of them end at last in culs-de-sac. A boatman must be skilled indeed to find his way. Hundreds of men have lost themselves forever in this reedy marshland.

Any trail or road into Barataria must, perforce, follow these winding streams, and the trails soon become a labyrinth among the swaying grasses. At long intervals *chênières* rise from the marsh—high mounds of shells covered with live-oak trees. These *chênières* are islands in the unending plain, and may be seen from miles away, dark irregular domes in a sea of blue-green light. The shore-line of the marsh is fantastic in its irregularity, and is cut by large bays into which the rivers and bayous empty themselves on their way to the Gulf.

As one sails southward from New Orleans, he traverses one curving bayou after another, bayous which widen into lakes and which close again into other bayous. At last this land of reeds and water is left behind, and Barataria Bay stretches out to the far horizon; one can smell the sea. The sky is an inverted bowl of gold and blue, and one can scarcely say where water ends and sky begins. Still the boat goes on, ever southward through the golden light, and at last a bright archipelago appears— low-lying islands, with masses of green trees and strips of shining sand. Beyond the islands one can see the blue waters of the Mexican Gulf; and one can hear the rustling of the palm-trees, and the pounding of the surf. Two

Barataria

large islands lie close together: these are Grande Terre and Grande Isle, and on clear days one may see, toward the west, another island—Chênière Caminada.

So it was in Lafitte's time, and so, in a sense, it remains to-day. It is true that there are settlements along the principal bayous, and fishermen and their families live in palmetto-thatched huts in isolated spots. But there still remains a vast realm of sea-marsh given over to gulls and terns and pelicans, and those other wild creatures which have lived and mated there from time immemorial.

This is a place of strange and passionate moods. Nature itself is capricious, changing in a moment from calm to storm. A warm, sweet breeze, which seems somehow subtly fragrant with orange flowers, blows all day from the south; yet, in a moment, it dies. A blanket of blistering heat falls upon the islands. Not a leaf stirs. The islands wait, silent, inert. And then, suddenly, the sun draws in and a whistling wind comes out of the Gulf; lightning flashes, and a tropical storm breaks with quick fury, lashing the twisted oak-trees with salt spray, and bending the tall palms away from the sea. Rain rattles down upon the wide leaves of banana-trees, a torrential downpour.

Then, as quickly as it came, the storm passes. The sun shines again with blinding light, and the wet green leaves of the banana-trees glitter like metal. The palms right themselves, dripping like slow-running fountains, and the soft breeze blows again from the south. Once

Lafitte the Pirate

more there comes that mysterious scent of orange flowers. And as the land is, so are the dwellers therein.

For fifty years before Lafitte saw it, men and women had been living on Grande Isle, and there was a cluster of houses half buried in the rank undergrowth. Dwarfed oak-trees, curiously twisted by the wind and their outer leaves scalded by the salt spray, grew in dense groves, their gnarled trunks leaning all in one direction, away from the sea. The houses were hidden beneath these trees, each house with its thicket of shrubs and oleanders which served as a protection from the wind that blew almost ceaselessly from the Gulf.

The houses were small and unpretentious. They contained only one or two rooms. The windows were closed, not with glass, but with heavy batten blinds which served as protection from the sudden storms. Orange groves dotted the island, the golden fruit shining like lanterns among the dark, polished leaves. And flowers grew before the doors of the cottages.

For half a century the smugglers' women had lived there, cooking, sweeping, laughing, crying, giving birth to children. . . . They were quiet, submissive women who obeyed the men blindly, women who had little thought beyond their men and their children.

Smuggling was only a part of the islanders' lives, for they were also trappers and fishermen. Their luggers made the long journey to the New Orleans market over

"BASSA-BASSA"—SHRIMPERS' HOUSES
IN BARATARIA

SMUGGLER'S COTTAGE ON GRANDE ISLE

Barataria

and over again, carrying loads of fish and shrimp and oysters. They knew these curving bayous as the average city-dweller knows the streets between his home and his office; the reedy labyrinths of Barataria held no mysteries for them. They had learned a hundred hiding places for themselves and their boats in the vicinity of the city, and when their luggers were loaded with contraband goods, rather than with fish, they felt safe from pursuit or attack.

For nearly fifty years, then, they had pursued their dual interests; it was an accepted thing. But the passionate moods of the islands had left their trace upon these men and upon the children born there; and they were as suddenly moved from careless mirth to quick and unreasoning fury as a child is moved from laughter to tears.

Then all was changed. A sterner, rougher group of men invaded the peaceful bayous and made homes for themselves among the islands. These newcomers were, for the greater part, seafaring men. They were men who had sailed under many flags, and war had taught them to hold life cheap. They were outlaws by choice and they had cast their lots upon the sea. Men of many races and many tongues—Spanish, French and Portuguese; men from the West Indian islands, men of mixed blood, negroes, Maltese, Catalans, outcasts and criminals, men from God-knows-where who had drifted from near and far to find a haven in the sea-marsh of Barataria.

A palmetto-thatched village had grown up around

41

Lafitte the Pirate

Jean Lafitte's house on Grande Terre; and while many vessels lay in the safe harbor behind the island, the men, resting between the voyages, slept and drank and caroused, or lusted after the women that they had brought with them.

Strange bits of description have come down to us of tropic afternoons on the islands. . . . Sunlight, white and blistering hot, streaming mercilessly upon those palmetto-thatched huts, sunlight which shone in long streaks between the openings in the rough boards of the walls; sunlight which stretched long fingers across the floor, further and further as the afternoon waned, and which fell at last upon sleeping men, lying, hairy and naked, upon the bare boards of the floor; sunlight which slanted, too, upon furtive women who crouched beside the sleeping men, women who preened themselves before bits of broken mirrors, as they forced their sweating bodies into gay dresses of damask and brocade, dresses sometimes stained with blood . . . for these were a part of the loot which the sailors had taken from the captured ships of Spain.

While the men slept through those torrid afternoons, Jean Lafitte swung lazily in his red hammock upon the veranda overlooking the Gulf. Sometimes he scanned the far horizon with the telescope which stood beside him. He had good reason to be pleased with life, for his community was prospering. Many rich prizes had been brought in, and the men, somewhat unruly at first, were

Barataria

beginning to realize that a certain restraint was necessary. Some of them were giving trouble though. There was Gambi, the Italian, for example. Gambi was a pirate and proud of it. He scorned the name of privateer, and had said—although not in Lafitte's presence—that he was master of his own vessel and he would do as he pleased, taking what loot he could, with no thought of the flag under which it sailed. But Gambi was at sea now and had been gone for two months. Perhaps he had met his match somewhere out there in the Caribbean. At any rate, he was not at Grande Terre and, for a time at least, he could stir up no dissension.

There was an ugly sound to that word "pirate." Jean Lafitte did not like it. And he was to swear, only a year later, that his men were privateers, "corsairs, not pirates." But the stubborn fact remains that while the vessels of the privateers brought in many slave-ships and other rich booty, the Baratarians were never known to have been troubled with prisoners.

Chapter VI

GAMBI AND DOMINIQUE YOU

In the autumn of 1811, Dominique You joined his fortunes with those of Lafitte.

You's life had been highly romantic. He was born on the island of Santo Domingo in the town of Port-au-Prince, and from boyhood had been a sea-rover. Finding himself in France at the time of the Revolution, he took part in several engagements prior to the establishment of the Consulate. He was an expert artillerist, and in time joined Leclerc, Napoleon's brother-in-law, in that unfortunate expedition against the negroes of Hayti in the revolt of 1802. When Leclerc's broken and defeated army returned to France, Dominique You engaged in privateering on his own account, but he found this occupation

44

Gambi and Dominique You

both "expensive and unprofitable" and was about to turn his attention to something else when he heard of Lafitte's establishment at Barataria. This community of corsairs, engaged in a similar pursuit, and possessing a ready market for the loot, seemed ideal. You sailed promptly for New Orleans to see for himself.

Lafitte gave him a warm welcome, for You's reputation for bravery had preceded him. The two men became warm friends; and before the year was out, Dominique was spoken of as "Jean Lafitte's favorite lieutenant."

He was a small man, but broad-shouldered and strong. His hair was light, but his face was tanned by sun and wind until his skin was like dark parchment. When angry it was said that he resembled "a ruffled eagle," but these outbursts of rage were rare. Ordinarily he was good tempered and as easily pleased as a child. He was known for his sense of humor and his love for practical joking. His bravery was proverbial.

Dominique You's vessel soon became one of the most dangerous privateers in the Caribbean. He sailed under the Bolivian flag, having bought letters of marque at Carthagena, letters granting him the right to "burn, destroy or sink any vessel belonging to Spain." When criminal charges were brought against him in 1814, it was charged that he was a pirate, and it was asserted that he preyed upon vessels of every nation. Perhaps he did, perhaps he did not, for You was never brought to trial; and with the records being what they are, it is next to impossible to

45

Lafitte the Pirate

say now, a century later. But one thing is certain: Dominique You's vessels brought in ship-load after ship-load of captured slaves to the harbor at Barataria; and the terrified savages, laden with chains, were dragged into the barracoon.

Prior to 1810, when that horde of buccaneers came swarming to Louisiana from the West Indian islands, the smugglers had bought their slaves from Cuban slave-traders. But under Lafitte's régime a simpler and more direct method of supply was arranged. Nowadays the ships from Barataria went well armed and well manned. They lay in wait, off the Cuban coasts, and intercepted the slave ships as they came from Africa. Instead of buying the cargoes, they stole them, and frequently burnt or scuttled the ships. Or sometimes the vessel with its cargo, but oddly empty of crew, was brought back to Grande Terre. And all this in the name of "Spanish prizes."

This kind of "purchase"—as the corsairs called it—had double advantage: the slaves cost nothing, and the long voyage to Africa was eliminated. Then too, with Lafitte's powerful connections in New Orleans, the slaves were easily sold. The community at Barataria was prospering.

Other richly laden prize vessels were brought into port: merchantmen, their holds filled with silks and spices from India. . . . At one time the Lafitte's storehouse was filled with "goods of English manufacture." All this, of course, from Spanish vessels . . . or so it was said.

Gambi and Dominique You

In December 1811, two whole cargoes of slaves were brought in and were "peddled" along the banks of the Mississippi from Natchez to Donaldsonville, and the authorities did nothing. The earlier proclamation of Governor Claiborne's had done little but advertise the activities of the smugglers; and now a steady stream of buyers came to the warehouse on Grande Terre. And in New Orleans, Pierre Lafitte took orders for slaves and merchandise, and promised delivery at any designated spot, with as much assurance as though he had been an honest merchant.

There can be little doubt that the public opinion in New Orleans in 1811–1812 was overwhelmingly in favor of Lafitte's establishment. It was an accepted thing. Jean Lafitte had many powerful connections in the city. Bankers bid against each other for his accounts, and for the accounts of Sauvinet, Lafitte's "man of business." Merchants, rich, and with high financial standing, had dealings with him. Jean and Pierre Lafitte were seen constantly in public places. Vincent Nolte, in his autobiography "Fifty Years in Two Hemispheres," writes of seeing Jean Lafitte and Dominique You "arm in arm with Auguste Davezac." Davezac was a rich merchant and the brother-in-law of Edward Livingston. And Edward Livingston was intimate friend and right-hand-man to Governor Claiborne.

John R. Grymes—our same "jolly Mr. Grymes" of the first chapter—had been appointed District Attorney, and any prosecution of the Lafittes or their men would have fallen upon him. But Mr. Grymes had other matters to attend to; and certainly he appeared to hold nothing against either of the Lafitte brothers, inasmuch as he was sometimes seen drinking coffee with either or both of them in Tremoulet's Coffee House.

Things were going well with the Baratarians—almost too well.

At this time Jean Lafitte seems to have been everywhere. He frequently made his appearance at country balls, well dressed and charming, and quite dazzled rustic society. His manners were courtly, his demeanor irreproachable. There are no tales told of the seduction of innocence. He was not after women but after business. His longest conversations were held with merchants and planters with whom he traded; but sometimes he took the young men away with him, thus securing recruits for his community among the islands. More than one simple Acadian youth left home and family to follow the fortunes of the sea. In the short space of a year, Jean Lafitte had built up a following that seems, a century later, incredible. He counted a thousand men in his establishment, and his depots for disposing of ill-gotten slaves and merchandise extended from New Orleans north to Natchez, east along the Gulf coast to Pensacola, and west along the Bayou Teche and other streams, to the banks of the Sabine River—now the border of the State of Texas. And he had warm friends everywhere.

Gambi and Dominique You

But he had enemies, too. In New Orleans there was an ever-growing group which feared and despised the Baratarians. Strange tales of piracies were whispered about. Too many ships were disappearing in the Mexican Gulf, ships which went to the bottom in clear, calm weather. Many dwellers of New Orleans feared to make the voyage to Charleston, Baltimore or Philadelphia. Then, too, the United States Customs officials were complaining; commerce was paralyzed, they said, by the smugglers, and by piracies committed in the Gulf and the Caribbean. But the stories and complaints were alike vague. There was no one incident upon which they could base a legitimate complaint. Every one knew that a flood of foreign merchandise was pouring into Louisiana, but no single offender had been apprehended.

Jean Lafitte was not unaware of his enemies, and he had no desire to give them opportunity to charge him with more than smuggling. Piracy was a word he disliked, and for that reason he decided to settle the matter once and for all, with his men.

There was Gambio the Italian, for example. Gambio —or Gambi, as he was called—had given trouble before, and was like to give trouble again; for it was known that he had attacked an American merchantman in the Gulf. Lafitte called a meeting of his lieutenants.

Ten men gathered in the brick house on Grande Terre, each man the commander of a vessel. Only a few names have come down to us, and we must be content with those.

49

Lafitte the Pirate

There was Dominique You, of course, and Jean Lafitte knew that he could trust You's loyalty; there was Beluche (or Bluche, as it is sometimes spelled), a man who was later to become a commodore in the Bolivian navy; Pierre Lafitte was there, and several others. Of the unruly corsairs, we know the names of only two: Gambi, and Louis Chighizola, both Italians. Chighizola, because he had lost part of his nose in a duel with sabers, was dubbed "Nez Coupé."

The council terminated with a violent quarrel. Nez Coupé was won over by Lafitte's argument, and promised that he would keep his hands off American vessels, at least; but Gambi would concede nothing. He denounced the rest as hypocrites and liars, saying that they voted in one way and acted in another. But the council outvoted him, and he could do nothing alone; for, had he done so, the others were strong enough to drive him, and his men, away from the islands, despite the fact that Gambi had been there before Lafitte ever set foot on Grande Terre. He left the meeting in a fury, and went outside to talk with his men, who like all the others, were waiting on the beach to hear the outcome of the meeting. Gambi called his men to one side, and they gathered and held secret converse.

It was nearly noon, and the tropic sun shone down with blistering heat. The crowd of sailors, waiting to hear the decision of their captains, was impatient. Jean Lafitte, looking out through the barred window of his house,

Gambi and Dominique You

knew that this moment must decide the future of his colony. Matters must be settled now, for all time.

Presently the group of Gambi's men came up the sandy beach and stood outside the door of the house. Gambi remained behind. The men were scowling and determined. One man, a young giant, barefoot, wearing a red handkerchief around his head and carrying a pistol in his hand, advanced. As Jean Lafitte appeared at the door, the bronzed young giant spat upon the sand, and shouted in a loud voice that Gambi's followers would take orders from no one, and that Lafitte could——

The sentence was never finished. There was the sound of a shot, and the sailor's pistol fell from his hand. He swayed for a long second above his swaying shadow, then fell forward on his face.

Above, on the veranda, Jean Lafitte stood, as impassive as an image. From his pistol a spiral of smoke curled upward.

"And that," as Dominique You said, years afterward, "put the fear of God into them."

Gambi's men said no more, but presently they went back along the beach, carrying the dead man with them.

Chapter VII

"CALLALOU"

"PIERRE LAFITTE," writes a contemporary, "worshipped unwisely at the shrine of Bacchus and Venus, and this eternal devotion undermined his great strength at last."

In our crude age when flowers of rhetoric are no longer considered indispensable, we would find it simpler to say that liquor and women had laid him low. The "stroke" which he had suffered, left his face distorted, but he appears to have felt no diminution in his physical strength or desire. Perhaps he regarded his illness as a warning that youth was passing—he was nearly forty years old—and that his days for excesses were numbered. For shortly after his recovery he threw himself into his old dissipations with renewed fervor. Nearly every night he was seen drinking with his old cronies at the bar of

"Callalou"

the Hôtel de la Marine; and frequently he remained away from the cottage all night, while Adelaide Maselari waited in vain, listening, there behind the batten shutters, for his returning footfalls in the quiet street.

She had hoped, during his illness, that he would remain faithful, for she had borne him a child and she had acted as a mother toward little Pierre; but now she was fearful, as such women have always feared, that her lover would take a younger mistress.

Her plight was common enough, so usual in fact, that her special form of heartbreak has become part and parcel of a Louisiana folk-song. Even to-day children are put to sleep to this old tune. It is called "Mamzelle Zizi." Here is a verse, written down as it is sung, in that patois called "Creole":

> Z'autres qu'a di moin, ca yon bonheur;
> Et moin va di, ca yon peine:—
> D'amour quand porte la chaine,
> Adieu, courri tout bonheur!
> Pauvre piti' Mamzelle Zizi!
> Pauvre piti' Mamzelle Zizi!
> Pauvre piti' Mamzelle Zizi!
> Li gagnin doulor, doulor, doulor—
> Li gagnin doulor dans cœur a li.

The translation would be something like this:

> Others say, it is your happiness:
> I say, it is your sorrow:

Lafitte the Pirate

When we are enchanted by love,
Farewell to all happiness!
Poor little Mamzelle Zizi!
Poor little Mamzelle Zizi!
Poor little Mamzelle Zizi!
She has sorrow, sorrow, sorrow—
She has sorrow in her heart.

This is but the first verse, and as the song progresses we learn that Mamzelle Zizi is sad at heart because another girl, Callalou, wears silk and madras, and we learn that:

Callalou's a shameless jade:
She wears dresses of brocade.

And so the song goes on, verse following pitiful verse, for Mamzelle Zizi knows only too well that the quadroon girl Callalou has taken her lover away.

Some have explained the old song by saying that Zizi is the white wife who sees herself supplanted by the quadroon girl; others say that Zizi is a quadroon mistress who sees herself superseded by a younger girl. But the song, oddly enough, has survived to this day as a lullaby; and generation after generation of Creole children have been lulled to sleep by its plaintive melody.

It may be that Adelaide Maselari sang that song to little Marie Josephe as she waited in vain for Pierre Lafitte's return. This is, of course, sheer and sentimental conjecture. But before long her fears were realized. The

54

"Callalou"

"Callalou" in this case was a quadroon girl of eighteen. Her name was Marie Louise Villars.

She was a *griffe,* the daughter of a white man and a quadroon mother. The mother herself had danced at the Quadroon Balls, not many years before, and had been taken under the protection of a wealthy sugar planter. Marie was the eldest child; next came a boy, and last another girl, Catherine. In 1811, when Pierre took Marie Villars for his mistress, Catherine was a child of thirteen.

The mother knew her business, and she had brought up her daughter in the best way she knew. Marie had a fair education, as good a one as her time and her race permitted. She was beautiful, golden colored, voluptuous; and she dressed magnificently. But at home in the cottage which she shared with her family, she was quiet and industrious. Her dresses, which cried Paris in every seam, she had made herself. Her mother had taught her to manage a household economically and well. She was that odd combination of industrious housewife and glamorous courtezan; she won Pierre Lafitte with her seductive beauty, and kept him by the simple device of making him comfortable. She asked little and gave everything.

Nor was this paragon of mistresses unusual. There were many like her. But perhaps this needs a word of explanation:

For more than forty years these balls for white gentlemen and women of mixed blood were held in New Orleans, well known to every one, and announced regularly by

Lafitte the Pirate

the town crier who rang his bell and shouted the news at the street corners. As early as 1788 we find Miro, the Spanish governor, issuing his curious edict that quadroon women should not appear in public wearing "silks, laces or plumes"—the only head-covering allowed them was the *tignon* or head-handkerchief. The reason for his strange decree was this: the white women of New Orleans were jealous of the beauty and the luxury of these daughters of joy. It was the custom for white spectators at theater or opera to sit in the parquet of the theater, while the "people of color" occupied the balcony and upper boxes; but in 1788 the magnificent toilettes of these swarthy beauties had put to shame the costumes of the white ladies in the tiers below. They had appealed to the governor, and he had acted accordingly.

These beauties were all children of white fathers and quadroon mothers, each generation lighter and lovelier than the last. They were not prostitutes in the strict sense, as these women were never promiscuous, but each one endeavored to find a white "protector," a man who would support her as her mother had been supported. Most of them were the mistresses of young Creole gentlemen of means and fashion; it was an accepted custom. It must be remembered that New Orleans was first a French, then a Spanish city, and these races did not look upon the quadroons as the Anglo-Saxons came to look upon them later. In addition, the last half of the eighteenth and the first quarter of the nineteenth century

THE QUADROON BALLROOM IS A CONVENT NOW

PIRATES MET IN THE OLD ABSINTHE HOUSE

"Callalou"

were not noted for a "high moral tone." Morality was to come into fashion with Victorianism. The Creole father, in the period which we are discussing, was willing enough to agree that his son take a mistress among these women. Working on the principle that "boys will be boys" he preferred that his son's mistress be under parental supervision. Usually the father furnished the money that set his son and the son's mistress to housekeeping in one of those houses described as "peculiar little dwellings near the ramparts."

Usually the connection terminated with the boy's marriage; sometimes it lasted for life, and many men kept up two establishments for years on end. If the relation terminated when the young man married, it was usual to have a money settlement, and some arrangement was made for the support of the children, if children had been born.

Needless to say, numerous tragedies grew out of such a society. There were suicides, duels, murders, usually well hushed-up and the motive concealed. The newspapers of the period are maddening with their hints, but the actual news stories are rarely found. There was a conspiracy of silence. The whole thing was "unmentionable"—a subject for eternal conversation among men, but barred forever from mixed company, and barred too from the public press. Were it not for numerous travelers who have left diaries, and who have described these balls in all their luxurious detail, we would know almost noth-

ing about them. But we do know that these balls—and the
matings resulting from such festivities—lasted from
1780 until 1830 or thereabouts.

It was a man's world, and the men enjoyed themselves. But one can well imagine the misery and despair
that such a state of society must have brought to many
women, both quadroon and white.

The girls born of these illicit unions followed the
fortunes of the mother; the girl chose the path that the
mother had followed, and her whole training was toward
pleasing some rich, white gentleman when she attained
maturity. Until the time of her début at the public ball
she was kept as chaste and as modest as possible. Her
beauty and her chastity were her chief attractions. After
her desertion by a white lover, she seldom made a second
like connection; she usually married a man of her own
race, and reared the children of her lover and the children of her husband in happy harmony.

The boys or "free men of color" as they were called,
were less fortunate. Sometimes their white fathers saw
to it that they were educated; oftener they had to shift
for themselves. They became carpenters, brick-masons,
plasterers, cabinet-makers; sometimes they became musi-
cians; occasionally fencing-masters. Most of them, as
we have said, married the former mistresses of the white
men, and thought nothing of it. Others, so light in complexion that they could pass for Spaniards or Frenchmen, left New Orleans and tried their luck in other cities;

"Callalou"

but if they succeeded in "crossing the line" into the white world they left forever those friends and relatives who knew their past histories.

In New Orleans, this "crossing the line" was, in the early nineteenth century, nearly impossible. The quadroon women were all Catholics and babies were baptised as soon as they were old enough. The Catholic authorities were strict in recording these births and baptisms. The white baptismal records and the records for negroes and all free people of color were kept entirely separate; there was almost no possibility of mistake. And I shall speak of this again later on, in telling what became of the descendants of Marie Villars and Pierre Lafitte.

The mother of Marie Villars considered her daughter extremely fortunate in securing such a protector as Pierre. For, despite his bad eye and slight facial distortion, he was a strong man, unmarried, and in the prime of life. It is true that he was more than twice the young girl's age, there were streaks of gray in his hair, and he was growing stout, but he was rich—oh, so rich!— and he was unlikely to marry. If Marie played her cards carefully she could secure independence for life.

And so it turned out. Pierre Lafitte established her in a comfortable house, well furnished, and for a time at least, settled down to a life of domesticity. How pleasant it was to return from those long trips to Barataria, and to find this haven of peace and contentment: a house of quiet simplicity, where the beds were piled high with mattresses of sweet-smelling moss, and covered with the whitest of sheets. How pleasant to lie there, pampered, flattered, by this beautiful submissive girl who was half woman, half child, a girl who hung on his words, trying in a hundred ways to please him, and who gratified every whim of his jaded taste. And always, in the background, the turbaned mother, dignified, quiet, moving noiselessly about the house, half servant, half friend. How pleasant it was to eat those toothsome Creole dishes which the mother prepared; gumbo with its snowy rice, chicken fricassee, cooked only as a quadroon woman can prepare it. The women flattered him, and treated him as though he were their benefactor and god—as indeed he proved to be. And the little girl, Catherine, looked at him with her large dark eyes.

Jean Lafitte came to the cottage, looked about, shrugged his shoulders, and accepted the situation. Perhaps it was just as well, he said, that the forge and shop be closed. Sauvinet and Laporte could look after affairs in town, and Pierre was needed now on Grande Terre. This cottage could serve for a rendezvous, a secret meeting place. And so it was arranged.

Adelaide Maselari and the children went to live with the Sauvinets.

Chapter *VIII*

THE ARREST

WHILE the Congress of the United States was debating the admission of the Territory of Orleans as a State, in a series of pyrotechnic wrangles, the people of New Orleans were thrown into panic early in January, 1811, by an insurrection of slaves.

The revolt had taken place in the Parish of Saint John the Baptist, on the left bank of the Mississippi River about thirty-five miles above the city. Hundreds of these negroes, many of them wild Africans lately brought to Louisiana, ran away from their masters, and formed a howling mob which brought terror to those white people living in the vicinity. Houses were fired, and white men and women fled for their lives. The negroes, emboldened at this success, formed themselves into companies, each with a commanding officer, and marched down the river bank toward the city, with beating drums and with flags displayed. At each plantation they forced other slaves to join them; and before they could be checked had burned no less than five plantation houses.

Most of the planters, warned by their own slaves of the approaching danger, fled with their families. But one of them, a man called Trepagnier (whose ruined dwelling still stands to-day on the river road some twenty-five miles from New Orleans), contented himself with sending his wife and children to safety, and he remained at home to protect his property. He provided himself with several loaded fowling-pieces and took his stand on the high veranda which encircled his house. From this point of vantage he could see for some distance, and there he remained alone, waiting for the mob to sweep down upon him.

In a short time he heard the frenzied shouts of the crowd, and presently the mob of negroes appeared at his front gate. But at the sight of his double-barreled gun which he leveled at them, and which they knew to be in the hands of an expert marksman, they wavered, drew back, and finally passed on. Shaking their fists, and whatever weapons they had with them, they shouted that they would return that night to cut his throat. More than five hundred negroes were in the crowd at the gate, but one determined man had held them off.

The Arrest

The poor savages did not go much further, for within a mile of the Trepagnier house, they were met by a strong body of militia under the command of Major Hilton who had come down from Baton Rouge, and a second group commanded by General Hampton who had hastened up with his men from New Orleans. At the first attack the negroes ran screaming with terror and despair. Sixty-six of them were slaughtered on the spot, and sixteen prisoners were sent to New Orleans for trial. The rest escaped to the woods and swamps, but many of them were badly wounded, and every day scores of corpses were discovered by the pursuers. Those sent to New Orleans were immediately tried and convicted. Their heads were cut off and placed high on poles at intervals along the river road, where they remained until destroyed by vultures and the elements.

At the formal investigation for causes for this slave insurrection, it was said that negroes lately smuggled into the Territory were at the root of the trouble. This statement, which found few enough to give it credence, was one more grudge which the authorities of New Orleans stored up against the Baratarians; for under Jean Lafitte's régime as leader of the privateering gentry, many hundreds of slaves had been smuggled into the vicinity where the revolt took place.

Claiborne appealed to the legislature for money and men, as he wished to send a punitive expedition to Barataria. But the request was disregarded. The danger of a slave insurrection was over, and the Creoles promptly forgot about it. Merchandise and slaves were cheap at Barataria, and things could drift along as they were for a while.

Nearly a year later, Claiborne succeeded in arousing the Customs officials to some extent. An organization was established—a sort of primitive Coast Guard service. Captain Andrew Hunter Holmes and a company of forty dragoons manned several small boats and set sail down the bayous toward Barataria.

Fishermen, bringing their wares to market, met them. The dragoons searched their boats but found nothing but shrimp and oysters. The next day the news of this was brought to Jean Lafitte. He laughed. Forty men, what were they against his establishment among the islands? He could muster nearly a thousand men if he needed them, and he knew that such a small force would never attempt to attack Grande Terre. Nevertheless, he fortified the island. Cannons were set up along the beach, and the walls of the rude fort were strengthened. He warned his *contrebandiers* that they must be careful in their journeys to New Orleans with smuggled goods. And to set an example for prudence and discretion, both Jean and Pierre Lafitte now headed these weekly expeditions to the city. They located the camp of Captain Holmes and his men without trouble, and, by the simple expedient of taking another route, managed to bring a record supply of contraband goods into New Orleans.

The Arrest

The early summer of 1812 passed almost without incident. In the little cottage near the ramparts, Marie Villars and her mother continued to take excellent care of the brothers when they wished to remain in town. Catherine, the younger sister of Marie, was fourteen years old now, and Jean Lafitte was her idol. She would sit for long minutes, motionless, looking at him with her large dark eyes. She amused him, as he thought of her only as a child, and he mistook her adoration for hero-worship. Her sister knew better; the child was in love. To tease her, Marie gave Catherine the nickname of "Jeannette."

In July, Marie Villars gave birth to a daughter. The baby was christened by Père Antoine in the Church of Saint Louis on August 28th, 1812. The record reads: "Rose Villars, daughter of Marie Louise Villars, *grifa libra,* concubine of Pierre Lafitte."

And the liaison continued. In the years between 1812 and 1825, Marie Villars presented Pierre Lafitte with seven illegitimate children, all of whom were properly baptised in the Church of Saint Louis, and their names written down in the registers for Free People of Color. As long as Pierre Lafitte lived he provided for Marie, and if he ever cared for another woman, there is no record of it.

But Jean Lafitte was strangely indifferent to women. Pierre, it is said, twitted him about it. And Jean replied: "Ah, brother, I must do the thinking for both of us!"

Lafitte the Pirate

On the night of November 16th, 1812, as the brothers were taking a small fleet of pirogues and skiffs filled with contraband merchandise through the moonlit bayous of Barataria, their convoy was surprised by Captain Holmes and his company of dragoons. Although the smugglers were armed, they were no match for the soldiers who outnumbered them two to one. In the smugglers' attempt to escape, one of their men was killed. The others were arrested, their goods were confiscated, and they were taken under guard to the city. A bond was arranged, and Jean and Pierre Lafitte and their men were released. Their trial was scheduled for November 29th. Captain Holmes wrote a brief report. Here it is:

Andrew Hunter Holmes of the United States army being first duly sworn deposeth and saith that said Andrew Hunter Holmes hath good reason to believe and doth suspect that the above-named persons did on or about the sixteenth of the present month and year, receive on board certain skiffs and pirogues to the number of five and aid and assist and abett in thus receiving a large quantity of foreign goods, which goods had been unlawfully put ashore from a certain vessel or vessels lying at anchor at or near Lake Barataria, and which goods were subject to revenue duties, the same not having been paid. And the said Andrew Hunter Holmes further saith that the said goods are of a value of three thousand dollars more or less, and further saith not.

(Signed) A. H. Holmes

Sworn to and subscribed before me this 19th day of November, 1813.

(Signed) Joshua Lewis

Chapter IX

ON SUNDAY AFTERNOON

SUNDAY, November 25th, 1812, was a day like spring: warm, golden sunlight followed a fortnight of chill and rainy weather. In consequence, the streets of New Orleans were filled with people—an excited crowd which buzzed with news of piracy in the Gulf of Mexico.

A man named Williams had arrived the night before and had told a tale of horror and bloodshed. He had been one of the crew of the American merchantman *Independence* of Salem, Massachusetts, returning from a voyage to the African coast. His vessel had put into Havana for repairs, and shortly after leaving the Havana harbor, had been attacked by pirates. The crew had been murdered and the vessel plundered. In the darkness, Williams had escaped—he hardly knew how—and had managed to reach the Cuban coast; there he had been picked up by a French sailing ship and had been brought to New Orleans.

Lafitte the Pirate

The story spread from lip to lip. Details grew more blood-curdling as the tale passed along. By afternoon the town was ringing with it: "Pirates! Pirates!" and some-times—although repeated in a whisper—"Lafitte!"

It was not an open accusation, for the Lafittes had many powerful friends, and there were too many who would resent coupling the name of Lafitte with such a thing. Jean Lafitte had said, over and over, that he warred only against Spanish vessels, and that his letters of marque from Carthagena permitted as much, as Spain was an enemy. But this story concerned an American vessel, and the English-speaking people of New Orleans were up in arms. A delegation of Americans, or so rumor said, had gone to see Governor Claiborne, and that even now, at this moment—which was four o'clock in the afternoon —they were closeted with the Governor and Mr. Grymes, the district attorney, and with the survivor, Williams.

The Place D'Armes was filled with a gay and vivid crowd, and little groups stood in earnest consultation, with frequent glances toward the closed, iron-grilled doors of the Cabildo where the conference was said to be taking place. The exciting news was all that was neces-sary to add zest to the holiday.

Lafitte's name had been drawn into the gossip in a peculiar way. If such an act of piracy had been com-mitted, said rumor, then Jean Lafitte must know about it, whether he approved or not, for he was "bos" (that was the word they used, and we have accepted it nowa-

E.H.Suydam
1920

A CAFÉ ON THE PLACE D'ARMES

BEFORE THE DOORS OF THE CABILDO

On Sunday Afternoon

days as part of our language). The smugglers and privateers had pooled their interests, with Jean Lafitte at the
head, and this "smugglers' trust" made it impossible for
other privateer vessels to operate in the Mexican Gulf!
Now this may, or may not, be true, but it was the gossip
in the Place D'Armes on that sunny Sunday afternoon
in 1812. And such gossip is rather significant, as it
implies an authority which is little short of complete.

The word "pirate" and the name "Lafitte" passed
back and forth through the crowd, sometimes jestingly,
sometimes seriously. Before the Church of Saint Louis,
a group of richly dressed men and women spoke in tones
hardly louder than a whisper, glancing now and then
over their shoulders toward the "Principal" or Cabildo.
The church doors stood open, and within the dim recess,
candles pricked the darkness with their pin-points of
light, and the devout knelt before the various shrines with
bowed heads.

But just outside the door the street vendors were
crying out their wares. Negroes squatted on the sidewalk
before the church, with their baskets of yellow oranges
beside them. The banana-sellers walked to and fro, carrying the golden-green fruit in baskets on their heads. A
group of children squealed with delight before a puppet
show. Negro women, in dresses of guinea-blue calico,
and wearing starched white aprons, moved through the
crowd offering pralines for sale—that sweet pecan candy
which was always a favorite in New Orleans. The ven-

dors of honey-flavored cakes offered their wares upon trays; and children came close, begging their parents to buy. Beside the iron palings of the square were the push-carts of those who sold *biere douce*—ginger-beer—cooled in tubs of water; and the sellers of *estomac mulatre,* that ever-popular ginger-cake, did a thriving business.

Moored beyond the levee were the schooners of the oystermen, low-lying, rakish boats with red sails; and along the levee-top were the booths where oysters on the half-shell were served, men and women standing in line to eat them as they were opened.

To-day one regarded the oystermen with additional interest, for they were Baratarians, and perhaps they know something of this story of piracy which grew as the hours passed; but if the Baratarians knew anything they gave no sign, and perhaps it was not good to inquire of them.

Indians, drunk and nearly naked, reeled by. Indian women followed patiently, peddling their red and green baskets. Black nurses led children along the levee, or along the palings of the square, letting them stop to watch the marionettes, or to sample the wares of the Greek sherbet vendor.

Within the square, beneath the sycamore-trees, men and women passed up and down in the afternoon promenade. Old gentlemen tottered along, leaning on their ebony canes, elegant in the costumes of their bygone youth, their golden shoe-buckles gleaming, silken knee-breeches shin-

On Sunday Afternoon

ing in the sun; they raised their black cocked-hats to ladies of their acquaintance, or stopped to converse with other old gentlemen, shaking back lace frills from their wrists, offering each other jeweled snuff-boxes.

Fresh-faced young girls, all dressed alike, walked two by two, on their way to church; and black-robed nuns, also in pairs, went with them, moving with downcast eyes past the gay and laughing group of dragoons that stood near the iron gates. The soldiers wore uniforms of red and blue, and their hats were ornamented with plumes. Matrons in gowns of silk or madras led prancing children along. City Guards in sky-blue uniforms and armed with formidable cutlasses paced by with measured tread. Young gentlemen in skin-tight pantaloons of yellow broadcloth, and with long coats of bottle green, stood about with negligent elegance as they discussed last night's opera or yesterday's *duello;* but an observer would have noticed that they were as vain as women, as they furtively adjusted their starched lace frills, or—with studied ease—threw back their coats to display vests of flowered silk. And for all their careless elegance they managed to keep a weather-eye out for the pretty girls who passed so demurely; nor did they overlook the charms of the gold-colored quadroon girls who swept past in their flowing silk gowns, looking neither to the right nor the left, and accompanied always by older, turbaned women of the same race. All New Orleans was there that day: men, women, children, stolid citizens and men who

71

Lafitte the Pirate

lived by their wits, saints and sinners, virgins and cour-
tezans.

The shadow of the church-spire was lengthening
across the grass when a startled murmur swept the crowd;
conversations broke off and there was a sudden silence as
the people stood looking, all in one direction.

Jean and Pierre Lafitte had appeared before the
church, and were strolling leisurely toward the iron gates
of the square. Had their entrance been timed, it could have
been no less dramatic. Did they know that their names
had been on every tongue that day? Or were they unaware of the story of piracy in the Gulf? Nobody could
say. Yet, somehow, the crowd could not but admire the
composure of these men, who chose this moment to
cross the Place D'Armes from church to levee.

Slowly they came, now and then exchanging a friendly word with this one or that. They were both faultlessly
dressed, Jean Lafitte in black as was his custom, and
Pierre resembling the other dandies in that he wore a
fashionable suit of green broadcloth.

The crowd made way for them, drawing back; and
the brothers walked on, past hundreds of staring eyes
and incredulous faces. There was a certain magnificence
about them. Jean Lafitte's tall body towered above most
of the men in the square. And even "that cross-eyed
Pierre" seemed more handsome than usual.

Ah, those Lafittes! Pirates or not, they had the manner and bearing of aristocrats. Creole women sighed, re-

On Sunday Afternoon

gretting momentarily, perhaps, the stolid respectability of their husbands. Young girls stared with frank admiration. Quadroon mothers whispered to their radiant daughters: "Ah, there are men for you!"

Somewhere near the center of the square an aged dandy raised his hat to the brothers with the polite formality of another era, and they, not to be outdone, removed their rakish black hats as they stopped a moment to exchange pleasantries. Those who stood near by could hear the words that were said.

The encounter lasted for only a moment, but as the brothers passed on a whisper spread through the square as a ripple spreads through a quiet pool. What superb composure! Did you hear what they said? They are on their way to General Humbert's birthday dinner.

On their way to a public dinner when the whole city rings with charges against them! *Magnifique!*

So splendid an impression the brothers made that day that the whole temper of the gossip in the square changed when they had gone. Probably, said the Creoles, there was no truth in the story that this man Williams had brought to New Orleans. What sort of cargo did this vessel carry from the African coast? Hah! No one had thought of that? These Americans from New England were no better than the Baratarians themselves, if the cargo of the *Independence* had consisted of the forbidden slaves. And for what else did one go to Africa?

Lafitte the Pirate

So, if privateers (not pirates, mind you!) had stolen the illicit cargo, it was no more than those Americans out of New England deserved. . . . So buzzed gossip, turning itself about like a weather-vane in the breeze stirred by the brothers Lafitte as they passed by.

And presently the desire for exciting news calmed itself, wavered, and was changed presently into a desire for home and supper. At sunset the crowd dispersed. The vendors packed their wares which remained unsold, and tramped away. One by one, the oyster-luggers raised their red sails and drifted with the river's current away from the levee, into the twilight.

Mr. Grymes, the district attorney, prepared a report upon what Williams had said: An American vessel, *carrying an illicit cargo of slaves,* had been attacked and destroyed by pirates in the Mexican Gulf. There was brief notice in the newspaper. The authorities read the report and did nothing. A week later, Williams had dropped from sight and the story was forgotten.

Chapter X

GENERAL HUMBERT'S BIRTHDAY DINNER

BUT if Jean Lafitte triumphed over public opinion in New Orleans that day, he did not fare too well at General Humbert's birthday dinner. For the celebration ended in something closely resembling a riot.

Jean Robert Marie Humbert was one of the strangest and most colorful personalities of old New Orleans. He was born in Rouvray, Lorraine, on November 25th, 1775, in humble circumstances. His father was a peddler of rabbit skins; but there can be no question of Humbert's intelligence or bravery. As a youth he enlisted in the army of the Rhine, and rose by gradations to the position of Major General in 1794, having taken part in every battle fought during the campaigns of Wurmser and the Duke of Brunswick. Humbert's attack on Lan-

Lafitte the Pirate

dau is sometimes spoken of by historians as "one of the boldest feats of arms ever recorded," and his success in the pacification of the Vendée, devoted to the Royalist faction, is highly praised, although most of the credit is given to Hoche, his ranking officer.

So it came about that, when the French Directory determined to attack England in her own stronghold, in 1798, Hoche and Humbert went at the head of expeditionary forces to Ireland to assist the insurgents in their attempts at independence. The attempt was a failure and led to untold butchery of the revolted peasantry. Humbert was forced to surrender to Lord Cornwallis at Ballymuck. As soon as an exchange of prisoners was effected, he returned to France and was given a command in the Army of the Danube, where in 1799, he was seriously wounded.

Two years later he was called to confer with Leclerc, Napoleon's brother-in-law, in regard to the expedition against the insurgent colony at Santo Domingo. One third of the force sent against that island was under the command of Humbert. On arrival he found the country in full revolt. The negroes, under the command of Toussaint L'Overture, had set up a government of their own, pillaging and firing the plantations of the whites. The European soldiers fell, almost immediately, victims of an epidemic of yellow fever. . . . Leclerc died; the French met with defeat everywhere and Napoleon was forced to recall the army.

General Humbert's Birthday Dinner

It was at this stage of his career that Humbert did a most preposterous thing: he took the widow of his late commander as his mistress. And the lady in question was none other than Pauline Bonaparte! This fact, plus the Republican tendencies and beliefs of Humbert, led to an open rupture with Napoleon, and Humbert was exiled to Brittany. There he gave full vent to his feelings, and was arrested for seditious utterances. He escaped and fled to Louisiana.

In 1812, he was fifty-six years old, and was a popular figure in New Orleans. Contemporaries describe him as a man of free and easy manner, tall, with a fine head, and a nose like a ripe strawberry. "He was given to dissipation," says one writer, "and in later years to habitual intemperance." He did not mingle in society, but sought the rough and ready comradeship of the cabarets. His favorite haunt was the café kept by Thiot, a Santo Domingan refugee, who had introduced a new beverage to New Orleans, known as *le petit Gouave,* which General Humbert had learned to drink in Port-au-Prince.

On that Sunday in 1812 he was celebrating his fifty-seventh birthday, and his friends and compatriots had planned a dinner for him at the Hôtel de la Marine. It was also the anniversary of some past military triumphs —now forgotten—and the occasion was to be doubly celebrated. The table was spread in the spacious dining-hall and to the party were invited the French convivial spirits of the city.

Lafitte the Pirate

The Baratarians were well represented. Jean and Pierre Lafitte were there, and so was Beluche, destined for naval triumphs of his own later on; Dominique You was there, laughing and jovial; Jean Baptiste Sauvinet, the banker, acted as master of ceremonies; Huette, the planter of Bayou Saint John, was there; and so was old Thiac the blacksmith. Paturzo, a Genoese, and Gambi the Italian were present, as was Nez Coupé with his scars. Jean Ducoing, later to become celebrated at the Battle of New Orleans, was among the guests, and so was Constanti, another Italian who left numerous descendants in New Orleans. There was Laporte, the dark, smiling bookkeeper for the Lafittes, St. Geme, a planter, and perhaps twenty more, who were all more or less connected with the mysterious establishment at Grande Terre.

The men had gathered around the table when General Humbert made his appearance in full uniform, with the tri-colored scarf of the erstwhile Republic across his chest. The men rose, cheering, when he entered, and he was escorted to an armchair at the head of the table.

What a dinner! Only to read of it nowadays is to feel the pangs of hunger. . . . Hors d'œuvres, crab gumbo, roast turkey stuffed with pecans and raisins, red fish cooked in white wine sauce . . . there was no end to it. And there were wines of rare vintage, plundered from some unfortunate Spanish galleon.

"There followed," says a contemporary writer, "the

78

bacchanalian song, the ribald jest, the pungent anecdote, adding zest to the revelry."

At last, when men were unsteady upon their feet, the patriotic toasts were in order, and it was then—as the party was beginning to turn into a debauch—that the unfortunate word was said.

Some unrecorded guest rose and proposed the health of General Humbert, who lolled, ribald and godlike, at the head of the table. The speech—which had been prepared beforehand—was a fulsome eulogy upon the old soldier, dealing minutely with his life and services.

On and on went the speaker, adding praise to adulation.

But some of the guests noticed that General Humbert had stopped smiling. His red old face grew crimson, and, when the speaker had ended, Humbert rose suddenly from his place, overturning his armchair.

The guests were sobered suddenly, as the deep voice of the old war-horse boomed out:

"Your words," he shouted, "remind me of what I was, and of what I am." He gulped and clutched his throat, "I must not remain here as an associate of outlaws and pirates. No, my place is not here!"

Then, turning to Beluche, whom he particularly disliked, he cried out a scathing denunciation, a mixture of strange oaths which threw the company into an uproar. It was the direct accusation of piracy and murder.

Bedlam was let loose. A score of daggers gleamed

in the candle-light, as the old man continued to beat upon the table and to shriek out his curses upon them all.

Things would have gone badly for him, but Jean Lafitte rose and stepped beside him, holding up his hand. Suddenly the old soldier burst into tears, and fell upon Lafitte's shoulder. One angry glance from Lafitte's dark eyes was sufficient to hold the men in check, and the old man was led from the room.

There was a murmur of rough voices: "He is drunk." But one man spoke slowly aloud. "No, his conscience spoke."

The very next day General Humbert had forgotten his outburst. By afternoon he was back at his old haunt in Thiot's café with his glass of *le petit gouave* before him.

But Jean Lafitte did not forget. He forgave the old General for what he said, but in the months that followed, he was seen no more at the Hôtel de la Marine.

Chapter XI

THE LAFITTES BECOME OUTLAWS

FOUR days after General Humbert's birthday dinner which ended so disastrously, the Lafittes were called for trial. Charges of smuggling were the only charges against them, but the brothers did not come to court. Instead came their man-of-business Sauvinet, to represent them.

The procedure is not clear, and one has only a handful of faded and incomplete documents from which to reconstruct the scene. We are lucky enough to have these, for they came to light only a year or two ago, and are now in the private collection of James B. Pelletier of New Orleans. Why these official documents were allowed to be removed from the records of the Louisiana District Court, I have no idea; but hundreds of similar papers

Lafitte the Pirate

have disappeared and that is why it is nearly impossible to follow any trial of that period to its ultimate conclusion.

However, what we have is interesting enough, for on November 29th, 1812, an examination of Captain Holmes was held in open court. He told his story and submitted to cross-examination; but who conducted the cross-examination, I cannot say. The document is so characteristic of the period, and so replete with details of the arrest of the Lafittes and their men that I give it here in its entirety:

Captain Andrew Hunter Holmes, being duly sworn, deposeth and saith that he with a party of between thirty and forty men was ordered out by Captain Woolsoncraft for the purpose of aiding the revenue officer in preventing the practice of smuggling by means of Lake Barataria. That he proceeded as far as twenty-five miles from the Mississippi without encountering any violation of the revenue law, that at that distance the sentry of the piquet guard of his detachment on the night of the 11th instant, hailed a pirogue and on his refusing to come to shore, fired his piece without injurious effect, that the pirogue then came to shore, and was found to have on board a small quantity of imported goods, that the deponent took out the goods and permitted the men to proceed on account of their behaving well after the capture; that about thirty-five miles from that place, at 10 o'clock at night, on the 16th inst., his party descried three or four sails upon the lake, which is the first large one after leaving the Temple, that his detachment immediately embarked and pursued them to the opposite shore, that when they saw deponent's party in pursuit

82

The Lafittes Become Outlaws

they took down their sails and applied their oars in an opposite direction, that in a few minutes deponent came within hailing distance, and to their question what boat is that, deponent answered: "United States torros," that deponent then hailed their boats and heard no answer given, then an answer was given, that they then told deponent's party if they came there, that they would fire into them and kill them every one, which were the words used in broken English, that the deponent seeing that they were very close to the shore ordered all his boats to land except one, that one was ordered with about fifteen men to row in front of their center and intercept their flight, that whilst in the act of landing their men crowded upon them, still menacing deponent's party with instant death if they left their boats, that is soon as deponent's party effected a landing they retreated, some to their boats, others from the lake to marsh, that when those who had run to the boats observed a large party in front and the rest of deponent's detachment drawn up on shore, they gave up the idea of retreating and surrendered, though with great reluctance, that after they began to surrender one boat attempted escape, that a party sent by the deponent to prevent it, fired into it, killing one man and took the rest prisoners, that all the boats were rowed across the lake to deponent's encampment, that but one boat as the deponent recollects was found to contain imported goods consisting of a large quantity of cinnamon and other articles, that deponent brought the whole of the goods and boats and all the prisoners except one who escaped a few miles above the city, that the names of the prisoners as they confessed themselves were: Jean Lafitte, Angel Rabello, Antoine Semet, Pierre Cadet, Pierre Lafitte, Michel Joseph, Andre Como. . . .

Twenty-five men were named, and all were charged

Lafitte the Pirate

with transporting smuggled goods. Then came the cross-examination of Captain Holmes, which is also given in its entirety.

Question: Were you sworn in as an inspector of customs?
Answer: Yes.
Q: Had either of the boats of the detachment a flag?
A: No.
Q: What time was it when you came up to the men in the pirogues?
A: He does not exactly recollect the hour, but it was bright moonlight.
Q: Did you on hailing the boats state to them that you were an officer of the revenue?
A: No.
Q: Did you hail them in English?
A: Yes, he did at about the distance of eighty yards, that they spoke very good English and threatened deponent's party in that language.
Q: What did you say relative to the conversation with Lafitte about the privateer?
A: That Lafitte said there was a privateer near Grande Isle and described her minutely as being of a considerable force.
Q: Were you in uniform at the time of the seizing of the boats?
A: That he was in the summer uniform which is a white roundabout without facings and pantaloons, but that the dress of his men, which was nearly the same as his own, was distinguishable from a citizen's dress by black bayonet and cartridge box belts, that many of them wore dragoon helmets with plumes and that some of them had on

The Lafittes Become Outlaws

their dragoon uniform, which is blue corded with white, and some the winter uniform, which is blue turned up with red, and that at the distance of thirty paces it was not possible to mistake them for citizens, except in disguise. Captain Holmes further states that he saw some of the men in the boats throw something overboard which had the appearance of a gun, that one of the men after being taken asked leave to regain his musket which he said he had for the purpose of killing ducks, that he found on board the boats two swords, very sharply ground, three fusils, charged and cocked, a dagger or small cut-and-thrust and a knife intended to be used as a dirk from the manner in which it was ground, that he does not know the kind of loading with which the fusils were charged, but that they still remain loaded.

(Signed) A. H. Holmes

Taken and sworn to and subscribed in open court, Nov. 29, 1812.

(Signed) Columbus Lawson, Clk.

What happened then is not clear, and the next document bearing on the case is dated four and a half months later! It is an elaborate and legally phrased petition by the State's Attorney, John R. Grymes.

To the Honorable Judge of the United States District Court in and for the District of Louisiana: The petition of the United States of America, by John R. Grymes, their attorney, in and for said district, most respectfully sheweth that Jean Lafitte, of the city of New Orleans in the district

85

Lafitte the Pirate

aforesaid is indebted to the said United States in the sum of twelve thousand and fourteen dollars and fifty-two cents, for this that all and singular the goods, wares and merchandise following to wit: Twenty-six bales of cinnamon, fifty-four linen shirts, three pieces of Russia sheeting, seven pieces of canvas, one bundle of twine, and one piece of handkerchiefs of the value of four thousand and four dollars and eighty-nine cents, being goods, wares and merchandise taken on board a ship or vessel arriving from a foreign port or place within four leagues of the coast of the said United States and unladed from out of the said ship or vessel before the said ship or vessel had arrived at the proper place for the discharge of her cargo or any part thereof, and without the authorization of the proper officer or officers of the customs to unload the same, were afterwards, to-wit, between the tenth day of November, 1812, and the seventeenth day of the same month at Barataria, in the district aforesaid, put and received into a certain boat or pirogue of which the said Jean Lafitte then and there had charge of command, with intent to violate the act of Congress in such cases made and provided, contrary to the form of the act of Congress in this behalf made. And also for this that all and singular the goods, wares and merchandise aforesaid of the value of four thousand and four dollars and eighty-nine cents as aforesaid and being goods, wares and merchandise laden on board a ship or vessel arriving from a foreign port or place within four leagues of the coast of the said United States and unladed from out of the said ship or vessel before the said ship or vessel had arrived at the proper place for the discharge of her cargo or any part thereof and without the authorization of the proper officer or officers of the customs to unlade the same were afterwards, to-wit, between the tenth day of November in the year 1812 and the seven-

The Lafittes Become Outlaws

teenth day of the same month at Barataria, in the district aforesaid, put and received into a boat or pirogue, contrary to the
act of Congress in this behalf made and with intent to violate
the same, in which same putting and receiving on board the
said pirogue of the goods, wares and merchandise aforesaid
to the intent aforesaid the said Jean Lafitte was then and there
aiding and assisting contrary to the act of Congress in such
case made and provided. By reason of all which premises and
by virtue of the act of Congress of the United States in such
case made and provided the said Jean Lafitte hath forfeited
and become liable to pay to the United States treble the value
of the said goods, wares and merchandise amounting to the
aforesaid sum of twelve thousand and fourteen dollars, fifty-
two cents. Wherefore the said attorney prays the consideration
of the court upon the premises that the same Jean Lafitte be
duly cited to appear and answer the plaint, and that judgment
may be rendered against him in favor of the said United
States for the aforesaid sum of twelve thousand and fourteen
dollars and fifty-two cents, with costs of suit, etc, etc.

(Signed) JOHN R. GRYMES, S. Atty. Lou. Dist.

It is evident that the pirate brothers, acknowledged
leaders of the affair, had been released on bond, but at
the three sessions of the court, April, July and October,
they failed to appear, wherefore the following writ typical of the six issued against the men:

Writ of the United States vs. Jean Lafitte.

The President of the United States of America. To the
Marshal of the Louisiana District or to His Lawful Deputy,
Greeting:

Lafitte the Pirate

You are hereby commanded, as you have often been commanded, that you take the body of Jean Lafitte that he be and appear before the district court of the United States for the Louisiana district to be holden at the city of New Orleans on the third Monday in October next, if the said court shall then be holden, or if said court shall not be holden on that day then on the first day thereafter on which said court shall be holden, to answer the complaint of the United States, and that he do file his answer on or before that day with the clerk of said court or judgment will be given against him be default and have you then and there this writ.

Witness the Hon. Dominick A. Hall, Judge of the said court at New Orleans, this 24th day of July A.D. 1813, and 38th of the independence of the United States of America.

(Signed) Columbus Lawson, Clerk

The papers in this collection make an imposing pile, and they tell an interesting story. Each of the six writs issued for the arrest of Jean or Pierre Lafitte are marked: "Not found in New Orleans." And there the matter rested, or so it appears.

However, there is no mistaking this fact: the Lafitte brothers were now definitely at war against Governmental authority. Their bonds were forfeited, and some one had lost twelve thousand dollars. Possibly it was Sauvinet, but more likely it was the Lafittes themselves. Twelve thousand dollars, although a large enough sum in those days, was nothing much to the Baratarians, for their affairs were prospering as never before. A steady stream of customers still came to the islands, and de-

FISHERMEN'S COTTAGES, GRANDE ISLE

GOVERNOR CLAIBORNE'S HOUSE,
TOULOUSE STREET

The Lafittes Become Outlaws

liveries of slaves and merchandise were made with regularity at Donaldsonville and along Bayou Lafourche. No expedition had approached Grande Terre, nor did there seem immediate danger of such an expedition being sent. Governor Claiborne had other things to worry about, and already New Orleans was beginning to fear an invasion by the British.

Chapter XII

OPEN DEFIANCE

THE Baratarians under the leadership of Jean Lafitte reached the height of their success in 1813; and, as Gayarre the historian somewhat grimly remarks, "their morals and general behavior declined in proportion to their gain in wealth and power."

The men at Grande Terre were a cosmopolitan lot: Portuguese, Spaniards, Italians, Frenchmen; deserters from the American Army and Navy; deluded boys—sons of respectable Louisiana families—who had followed the glamorous Lafitte in search of money or romance or adventure; there were also many half-breeds, and negroes from Santo Domingo, the last named a degenerate and bloodthirsty crew. There were no race distinctions among the islanders; the form of government was highly com-

Open Defiance

munistic. Lafitte was the "bos," but each man had a share in the distribution of prize-money and other loot. In 1813, it is said that each man's quota was more than five hundred dollars a month, and that the officers received many times that sum. No one could say just how much money the Lafitte brothers had, but they were very rich.

Nowadays, when a prize ship was brought into the harbor behind Grande Terre, there was a fête on the island at night; singing and ribald laughter, roistering and drunkenness upon plundered wines and brandies. Torches flared out over the dark water, and the men lay about on the beach, sodden with the gratification of every appetite. Grotesque and horrible legends have come down to us: tales of women dragged screaming from aboard the captured prize ships; women whose lives had been spared when the crew of the luckless vessel had been murdered; women who now met a worse fate among those brutal and drunken sailors. The horror tales are but fragments—a strangled scream, a woman, nude and bloodstained, dragged by her hair across the sandy beach, only to disappear into the black shadows which lay beyond the flaring torchlight . . . a mutilated corpse buried before daylight in a shallow grave in the sand. . . .

These are but legendary tales, repeated from generation to generation: there are no written records of such things, and the legends remain unverified. But some such stories were current in New Orleans as early as 1813, and there were some who believed them, whether true or not. The classic phrase of pirates might be used in this connection: Dead men tell no tales. Nor do dead women.

But to turn from legend to fact. The men were not easily controlled, and sometimes they got out of hand altogether. In their excursions to New Orleans, where many of them went to squander their prize-money in the grog-shops and cabarets and upon the women of the town, the Baratarians gave ever-increasing trouble to the City Guards. They paraded through the muddy streets late at night, shouting their drunken songs and obscenities. Sometimes they engaged in free-for-all fights with the Mississippi flatboatmen, or "Kentuckians" as they were called; and here the Baratarians met their match, for the boatmen were strong men and as eager for a fight as the islanders themselves. Riots, following such encounters, ended sometimes in the injury or murder of a respectable citizen of the town who had taken no part in the fray, but who was merely unfortunate enough to be in the vicinity when the fighting began.

Robberies were common; numerous incendiary fires were laid at the door of Lafitte's men. An ever-increasing number of citizens of New Orleans were becoming incensed at this lawlessness.

But the prize ships continued to be brought to Grande Terre with regularity, and the warehouse was filled to overflowing with valuable merchandise. Weekly deliveries of contraband goods still came to New Orleans,

Open Defiance

and convoys of sailing boats and swift pirogues went each week through Bayou Lafourche to the rich plantations along its banks and beyond to Donaldsonville, on the Mississippi River. And other groups of boats manned by the Baratarians went nearly as often to the plantations and trading posts along Bayou Teche.

Early in 1813, between the time of Jean Lafitte's first arrest and the date set for his trial, a public auction was held at a *chênière* called "The Temple" deep in the swamps. The auction was advertised by handbills signed by both Lafittes, and stated plainly that both slaves and merchandise were for sale. The time and the place were given, and scores of merchants and planters came to bid and to buy.

"The Temple" was an ancient Indian mound of white shells, where tall live-oak trees grew. It was a beautiful spot, and was believed to have been the scene of human sacrifice when Indians gathered there in bygone years for their ceremonials. But now it was used as a storehouse and auction-place. Lafitte's men had erected a platform there in the shallow waters of the marshland; and here they unloaded their boats and spread out their merchandise. This *chênière* was much nearer New Orleans than Grande Terre, and was within easy reach of those who wished to attend the sale of contraband goods. Buyers came flocking, and the auction was a great success. Each day the Baratarians were growing bolder. Another auction was announced.

Lafitte the Pirate

A change had come over Jean Lafitte. He was more morose, and quicker to anger. He was more arrogant now, and cared less for public opinion. He had been declared an outlaw, and as such he was playing the game. He is quoted as saying: "I would as soon drown in ten feet of water as in six!"

On March 15th, 1813, before Lafitte's bond had been forfeited, Governor Claiborne issued this proclamation:

WHEREAS I have received information that upon or near the shores of Lake Barataria, within the limits and Jurisdiction of this State, a considerable Banditti composed of Individuals of different nations, have armed and equipped several Vessels for the avowed purpose of cruising on the high Seas, and committing depredations and piracies on the Vessels of Nations at peace with the United States, and to the great injury of the fair trade of the Public Revenue;—And whereas there is reasonable ground to fear that the parties thus waging lawless War, will cease to respect the persons and property of the good Citizens of this State;—I have thought proper to issue this my Proclamation hereby Commanding the persons engaged as aforesaid, in such unlawful acts to cease therefrom and forthwith to disperse and separate;—And I do charge and require all officers civil and Military in this State, each within his respective District, to be Individual engaged as aforesaid in the violation of the Laws;—And I do caution the people of this State, against holding any kind of intercourse, or being in any manner concerned with such high offenders;—And I do also earnestly exhort each and every good Citizen to afford help, protection and support to the officers in suppressing a combination so destructive to the Interests of the United States and of

Open Defiance

this State in particular, and to rescue Louisiana from the foul reproach which would attach to its character should her shores afford an asylum or her Citizens countenance, to an association of Individuals, whose practices are so subversive of all Laws human and divine, and of whose ill begotten treasure, no Man can partake, without being forever dishonored, and exposing himself to the severest punishment.

> Given under my hand, & the Seal of the State at New Orleans on the 15th day of March in the year 1813, and in the 37th of the Independence of America.
>
> (Signed) WILLIAM C. C. CLAIBORNE

When the news of the governor's proclamation reached Grande Terre, Jean Lafitte snapped his fingers. Claiborne was a coward, he said, and dared not call the Lafittes by name, although even now he, Jean Lafitte, was awaiting trial. Well, Spain and England were his enemies, and now he was outlawed by the United States. So be it.

Let them all come.

Chapter XIII

TWO REWARDS ARE OFFERED

HE did not forget, though, to hold his old friends and
to make new ones. There are scores of stories of Lafitte's
generosity, and from among them I select one that I
know to be authentic; it is a part of Martha Martin's
memoir. This unpublished diary came into my possession
when I was collecting material for an earlier book—
"Father Mississippi" and I used it in its entirety at that
time. But now I shall quote but a fragment which deals
directly with Jean Lafitte. Mrs. Martin was the wife of a
Kentuckian who came to Louisiana and bought a plantation on Bayou Teche in 1810. The following incident
seems characteristic of Lafitte's liberality:

Two Rewards are Offered

During the war with England, the planters often could not obtain certain articles that were necessary for them to have on the plantation. Mr. Martin, Mr. Patten, Mr. Caffrey and others concluded to take a schooner and go where they had heard they could obtain those things needed.

Having purchased what they wanted and were returning home, the second night a terrible storm came upon them. They dropped anchor and remained until daylight. The pilot thought they might with safety leave, but very soon they found the vessel sinking. They threw a portion of the iron out, but still they found there was no hope of saving the boat. They had a yawl and being only about one half mile from the land, all got in the yawl except three or four. Mr. Sumner, Mr. Patten, the pilot, and a servant of ours remained on the vessel, as a part of it was out of the water.

After getting on the beach, Mr. Caffrey and one of the sailors returned to the vessel where they found Mr. Sumner with his arms around a plank, drowned, while Mr. Patten and the pilot were not to be found. The servant was hanging on the mast perfectly insensible. They brought the servant and the body of Mr. Sumner on shore. Mr. Sumner was buried on the island and the servant recovered. They were all left without any provisions and only a small yawl in which to get home, so those remaining of the party left the next morning, making slow progress.

Two days later, they saw some vessels ashore. They immediately made for them, but Mr. Martin concluded that it was most prudent for one of them to go and ascertain who they were. He went himself and found it was Lafitte the pirate. He made his situation known; immediately Lafitte sent for them and treated them with all the kindness possible, taking them aboard his vessel and giving them a bountiful breakfast.

Lafitte the Pirate

Mr. Martin related their unfortunate disaster to him and how far they were from home. Lafitte ordered a schooner made ready at once, putting in provisions and all that was necessary; and in fact, it was just what they had lost by the storm. He enquired of Mr. Martin if he had a family: he replied: "I have a wife and child," so he sent me a demijohn of Madeira wine, and the first pineapple cheese I ever saw. He told my husband that the schooner and contents was a present from him. . . .

It was several days before they reached home. My husband had lost his hat when leaving the sinking vessel, but Lafitte supplied him with a cap and cape attached, which was very acceptable in December (1812). Mrs. Sumner, my next door neighbor, was with me the evening before they arrived home. We were fearful of some accident, they being gone so much longer than we expected, but the sad news came soon enough for her. I have never witnessed greater grief and sorrow, for long did she moan for her dear husband. His brother sent out for Mr. Sumner's remains, which were brought back and buried at his home in 1813 . . .

In June, 1814, we left to visit my father in Nashville, Tennessee, driving in carriages. . . . The second day of our journey we reached Berwick's Bay and we learned that the pirate Lafitte had been taken prisoner and was sent to New Orleans, but very soon had escaped. . . . A large reward was offered for him. . . . I think he certainly had many good friends. . . . We spent the night at an inn near Berwick's Bay. . . . As we went down stairs the next morning, a servant approached us. I think he was a Spaniard. He enquired if that was Mr. Martin and said that a gentleman wished to see him. Mr. Martin took me in the dining room and then followed the servant. Our breakfast was ready in a few minutes. The lady remarked: "Will

Two Rewards are Offered

you wait for your husband?" and I replied: "He will be in soon." I sat down and commenced eating and after awhile Mr. Martin came in. The lady sent upstairs for my baby. Soon after breakfast we left. I think we were twenty-five miles on Bayou Lafourche from Donaldsonville. When we arrived there, Mr. Martin told me that he had business with some gentlemen which would delay him a short time.

While we were there we had our dinner, and I enquired often of Mr. Martin who it was that he stopped at Donaldsonville to see, but he evaded answering me. Some time after he told me it was Lafitte the pirate that had been concealed in the inn and that Lafitte had wished him to take some letters to Donaldsonville. On entering the room Lafitte looked at him saying: "Sir, I think I can trust you." Recognizing Lafitte, Mr. Martin replied: "You can. Your kindness to me cannot be forgotten and whatever I can do for you will be done with pleasure."

Lafitte then said: "You will deliver these letters to such gentlemen as I direct, living in Donaldsonville." He then gave Mr. Martin all the information necessary and handed him the letters saying: "Sir, I have learned you were here this morning and I immediately concluded to put these letters in your charge, and I feel that they will be safely delivered."

Mr. Martin was always quiet on that subject. . . .

When the Martins first enccuntered him, Jean Lafitte was at the peak of his success; two years later, when they met again, he was hiding at a country inn. But in the meantime many things had happened.

The Baratarians had preyed once too often upon British merchantmen, and on June 23rd, 1813, a British

Lafitte the Pirate

sloop of war anchored off the outer end of the channel at the mouth of Bayou Lafourche and sent her boat loaded with marines to attack the pirates. On entering they found two privateers lying close in to Last Island, and the Englishmen attacked at once with great bravery—for theirs was the smaller force. But the pirates stood their ground and drove them back with severe loss. After much firing on both sides, the English officer, seeing that he was getting the worst of it, withdrew his ship, which soon hoisted sail and left the privateers in possession of the anchorage.

This, as far as we know, is the only attempt made by the English to dislodge the Baratarians.

As the year progressed, Lafitte's men became more and more aggressive. On the 14th of October, a company of dragoons under the command of Walker Gilbert, a Revenue Officer, caught Jean Lafitte and his men with a shipload of contraband goods in the marshes near New Orleans.

Only a year before, Lafitte had surrendered to Captain Holmes, but this time he ordered his men to resist arrest. A skirmish ensued and Gilbert and his men succeeded in taking possession of the schooner and its contents; but almost immediately the Baratarians attacked again, wounding one man severely, and routing the soldiers. Then the Baratarians, at Lafitte's command, proceeded on their way with the contraband merchandise, leaving the wounded man in the swamp.

Two Rewards are Offered

This was too much. Claiborne had already appealed to the State Legislature for money and men to destroy the settlement at Grande Terre; but the Legislature did nothing and his request was neglected and forgotten.

Now he issued another proclamation, this time naming Jean Lafitte as the leader and offering a reward for his capture.

WHEREAS the nefarious practice of running in Contraband Goods, which has hitherto prevailed in different parts of this State, to the great injury of the fair trade, and the diminution of the Revenue of the United States has of late much increased—

And Whereas, the violators of the Law, emboldened by the impunity of the past trespasses, no longer conceal themselves from the view of the honest part of the community but setting the Government at defiance in broad daylight, openly carry on their infamous traffic; and Whereas it has been officially known to me that on the fourteenth of last Month a quantity of contraband goods seized by Walker Gilbert, an officer of the revenue of the United States, were forcibly taken from him in open day at no great distance from the City of New Orleans by a party of armed Men, under the orders of a certain John Lafitte, who fired upon, and grievously wounded one of the assistants of the said Walker Gilbert; and although process has been issued for the apprehension of him, the said John Lafitte, yet such is the countenance and protection afforded him, or the terror excited by the threats of himself and his associates, that the same remains unexecuted.—

And Whereas the apathy of good people of this State, in checking practices so opposed to morality, and to the Laws and

Lafitte the Pirate

interests of the United States, may impair the fair character which Louisiana maintains, and ought to preserve as a member of the American Union;

I have thought proper to issue this my Proclamation, hereby strictly charging and commanding all officers of the State, Civil or Military, in their respective departments, to be vigilant and active in preventing the violation of the Laws in the premises, and in apprehending and securing all persons offending therein; And I do solemnly caution all and singular the Citizens of the State, against giving any kind of succour or support to the said John Lafitte and his associates but to be aiding and abetting in arresting him & them, and all others in like manner offending, and I do furthermore, in the name of the State, offer a reward of five hundred Dollars which will be paid out of the Treasury, to any person delivering the said John Lafitte to the Sheriff of the Parish of New Orleans, or to any other Sheriff in the State, so that he the said John Lafitte may be brought to Justice.—

> In testimony whereof, I have caused the Seal of the State, to be hereunto affixed.—
>
> Given under my hand at New Orleans on the 24th day of November 1813. & of the independence of the United States the thirty-eighth.

By the Governor
(Signed) L. B. MACARTY, Secy. of State.

> (Signed) WILLIAM C. C. CLAIBORNE.

The Governor's proclamation was printed and posted in public places. And it caused open astonishment in some quarters; for certain influential men in New Orleans had

Two Rewards are Offered

boasted that Claiborne dare not bring Lafitte to justice. Nevertheless, a reward was now offered for his capture.

But when Jean Lafitte appeared in the streets of the city the next day no one molested him. The Creoles could not but admire his indifference to danger; and when he was seen perusing the proclamation and smiling, they were amused by his nonchalance.

Two days later a similar proclamation appeared at the same places where the Governor's had been shown. This time it was a clever parody of that official's language, and the names had been reversed. This time a reward of fifteen hundred dollars was offered for the arrest of William Charles Cole Claiborne, and for his delivery at Grande Terre. The proclamation was signed by Jean Lafitte.

The people of New Orleans could not restrain their mirth.

What a man!

Chapter XIV

PIERRE GOES TO JAIL

THE Creoles of New Orleans laughed at the wit of Jean
Lafitte, but Governor Claiborne was not amused. It may
be that he smiled for a moment when Lafitte's "proclamation" was shown to him, for he was a man not without humor; but there were urgent matters to consider,
matters even more serious than open defiance by the
Baratarians.

The dispatches from Washington were alarming; the
war with England was not going well, and there was a
growing certainty that the British would attack New Orleans. Detroit had surrendered in 1812; and although the
Constitution had destroyed the English vessel *Guerrière*

104

Pierre Goes to Jail

and had won other victories, the *Wasp* and the *Frolic* had torn each other to pieces; and, at the approximate time that Lafitte's men had driven off the English in their skirmish at the mouth of Bayou Lafourche, James Lawrence had been crying "Don't give up the ship!" as the American *Chesapeake* was taken by the British *Shannon*. The navy of the enemy was threatening the Atlantic seaboard; on land, the British had aroused the Indians against the Americans and bitter warfare was raging. The Federal Government was too occupied with its troubles nearer the Capital, to give aid to far-away Louisiana.

In the month of September, 1813, the population of New Orleans learned that the war with the Creek Indians was assuming a terrifying aspect. Fort Mims, some twenty-five miles from Mobile, had been taken by the savages; three hundred and fifty men, women and children had been brutally massacred. Many slaves had escaped from various plantations and had joined the Indians. It was feared that the Choctaws would soon become hostile. Extreme vigilance was necessary. Claiborne sent a circular to all the militia colonels, urging them to be ready to meet any emergency. He even made an arduous trip throughout the State, to prepare what defense he could. He had just returned from this trip when he found it necessary to issue his proclamation against Jean Lafitte, and to offer a reward for his capture.

The month of December came without any of the expected assistance from the Federal Government, and the year was closing with more threatening rumors of an approaching invasion of Louisiana. "The Federal Government," says Gayarré, "was either deaf to his repeated entreaties for men and munitions of war, or had not the power to grant the desired supply."

General Flournoy, in command of the United States forces on the Mississippi River, informed the Governor that he "could not conveniently concentrate within the State more than seven hundred men." Claiborne was at his wits' ends. . . . The only good news came shortly before Christmas: General Andrew Jackson of Tennessee, with a body of regulars, had pursued the Indians from the neighborhood of Mobile and had defeated them at Horseshoe Bend on the Tallapoosa River. Six hundred Indians had been killed and the rest scattered. . . . There was also the bad news that Napoleon was retreating from Moscow and suffering tremendous losses.

On New Year's Day, handbills were scattered through the streets of New Orleans, announcing that Jean and Pierre Lafitte would hold an auction at "The Temple" on January 20th. Four hundred and fifteen slaves were offered for sale, and also a quantity of "fine foreign merchandise." Claiborne held immediate conference with the United States Collector of Customs. There was little enough that they could do, nevertheless, the Collector sent the small force that he had to stand guard at the auction-place in order to "defeat the purpose of these law infractors." The gesture seems mild enough. The Collector had not reckoned upon the determination of the Baratarians.

On January 24th, came the news that Stout, a temporary inspector of the revenue, who, with twelve men, had been stationed at "The Temple," had been attacked by Jean Lafitte and his companions. Stout had been killed; two others had been fatally wounded, and the rest of the men were held prisoners. The auction had been a great success. Scores of buyers had come from various parts of the State. Every slave had been sold.

The Collector's report to Claiborne is extraordinary in its mildness, and ends in this calm fashion: "It is high time that these contrabandists, dispersed throughout the State, should be taught to respect our laws, and I hold it my duty to call on your Excellency for a force adequate to the exigency of the case."

Claiborne had no force of men to offer, but he sent a copy of the Collector's statement to the Legislature which was then in session. He sent, also, his own request for money and men. Claiborne's letter shows his helplessness. He says that, if the Baratarians are to be driven out, the State of Louisiana must do it, as "the General commanding the Federal troops in this district has declared that he finds it inconvenient to the service to withdraw at the moment any part of them from the important and exposed posts which they now occupy."

The letter is so curious that it is worth noting:

Lafitte the Pirate

My present powers are doubtless competent to the ordering
of a detachment of militia on this service [he continues], but
I owe it to myself and to the State to guard against even the
probability of a miscarriage. For it would be indeed a melancholy occurrence, if the men detailed for this duty, encouraged
to disobedience by the late conduct of some militia corps, should
furnish evidence of the inability of the Executive to enforce,
on this occasion, the supremacy of the laws. I therefore recommend this subject to your immediate consideration.

The late conduct of the militia corps sent against the
Baratarians had been indeed "a melancholy occurrence,"
for Jean Lafitte had bought them off. As one sentimentalist of the period remarks: "The brave leader of the Baratarians had spared their lives, loaded them with costly
presents and had allowed them to return safely to New
Orleans." All of which is very nice, but it left Claiborne
in an embarrassing position, doubtless.

The evil requires a strong corrective [he goes on]. Force
must be resorted to. These lawless men can alone be operated
upon by their fears and the certainty of punishment. I have not
been able to ascertain their numbers . . . but they are represented to be from three hundred to five hundred, perhaps
more . . . their principal place of depot for their plunder, an
island within the Lake Barataria, is defended by several pieces
of cannon. And, so systematic is the plan on which this daring
attempt against the laws of our country is conducted—so numerous and bold are the followers of Lafitte, and, I grieve to
say it, such is the countenance afforded him by some of our

citizens, to me unknown, that all efforts to apprehend this high offender have hitherto been baffled.

The Legislature listened to the reading of Governor Claiborne's letter, and turned it over to a committee. Nothing happened.

In the meantime, Lafitte, "with the utmost unconcern," was in the daily habit of sending his contraband goods to Donaldsonville, a town situated at the junction of Bayou Lafourche and the Mississippi River. Nowadays, armed bodies of men went with every consignment.

"His confidence," says Gayarré, "seems to have been well founded, since the legislature, on account of want of funds, postponed to some more opportune moment the organization of the military expedition which Claiborne had so earnestly solicited."

Other writers of the period are less lenient in their judgments: "There is little doubt," says Martin, "that the ill-gotten money of Lafitte played its part in the Legislature's disregard of Claiborne's request." All of which has a very modern flavor.

On March 2nd, Claiborne wrote again to the General Assembly:

I lay before you a letter which was addressed to me on yesterday by Colonel Dubourg, the Collector for the District of Louisiana, from which you will perceive the great and continued violations, within this State, of the non-intercourse, the

Lafitte the Pirate

embargo, and other laws of the United States, and the necessity of affording to the officers of the revenue the support of an armed force whilst in the discharge of their duty . . . and for such aid as will enable the officers of the revenue to fulfill their obligations. I entreat you therefore, to furnish me with the means of co-operating, on this occasion, with promptitude and effect. It is desirable to disperse those desperate men on Lake Barataria, *whose piracies have rendered our shores a terror to neutral flags and diverted from New Orleans that lucrative intercourse with Vera Cruz and other neutral ports which formerly filled our Banks with rich deposits.* It is no less an object to put an end to that system of smuggling which exists to the disgrace of the State, the injury of the fair trader, and the diminution, as I am advised, of the circulating medium of this city in so great a degree as is likely to produce serious commercial embarrassments, then it is important above all to prevent breaches of the embargo law, and to make the projects of those traitors who would wish to carry supplies to the enemy. To enable me to accomplish these ends, or at least some of them, I ask for authority to raise by voluntary enlistment a force of not less than one captain, one first lieutenant, one drummer, one fifer, and one hundred privates, to serve for six months unless sooner discharged, and to be employed under the orders of the Governor in dispersing any armed association of individuals within the State, having for object the violation of the laws of the United States, and to assist the officers of the revenue in enforcing the provisions of the embargo, non-intercourse, and other acts of Congress. The officers, non-commissioned officers and privates to be entitled to the same pay, rations and emoluments as are allowed the troops of the United States, and to be subject to the rules and articles of war as prescribed by Congress. . . .

Pierre Goes to Jail

Again the Legislature did nothing. They talked of other things, and humiliated Claiborne by rejecting five successive nominations which he offered to fill a vacancy on the Supreme Bench. The Senate was openly hostile to the Governor, and gave out a statement that such an organization of militia was not to be forthcoming as there was no law to authorize, "and no necessity to justify the requisition." One of the newspapers denounced the Governor as "the tyrant of the day." He found himself almost powerless.

On the 14th of April, Congress repealed the embargo and non-importation laws, but it was difficult for the commerce of New Orleans, under the circumstances, to recuperate quickly. In the course of the month the banks of the city suspended payment. . . . About the same time, official reports of the fall of the French Emperor reached Louisiana. There was great excitement, and a new fear was expressed: England, now released from her great antagonist, would be left free to continue her war against the United States. A report reached New Orleans that, as one of the conditions of peace, England would demand the retrocession of Louisiana to Spain, her ally; for Spain had protested against the cession of Louisiana by Napoleon to the United States. Claiborne, in a letter to the Secretary of the Navy, wrote:

I observe with regret that many citizens of the State seem to think that their connection with the United States has become precarious. For myself, however, I have not hesitated to assert that my country will never consent to sever the Union, and that the power does not exist that can deprive the United States of the sovereignty of Louisiana.

Claiborne had failed again in his attempt to destroy the Baratarians. A gibe in a French newspaper set the whole city laughing; and, in their mirth, the people forgot that any ethical issue was involved, forgot that smuggling was ruining the business of honest merchants, forgot that money diverted from its usual channels had caused banks to suspend payment—forgot everything, in fact, except that a Frenchman had triumphed over the American governor. The Creoles found that fact extremely amusing.

Force failing, Claiborne tried strategy. While the city was still rocking with laughter, he called a meeting of American merchants and bankers; a friendly Grand Jury was chosen. Before this jury came a long line of witnesses, who swore to acts of piracy by Lafitte's men. The investigation was conducted with the strictest secrecy, and the records are so incomplete that it is almost impossible to determine exactly what was done. It is evident that there was a fear that witnesses would be intimidated—then as now. Indictments were found against both Lafittes, and against their two lieutenants "Johnness" and "Johnnot." Why these names were used, I cannot say, as it was generally understood that "Johnness" was Beluche, and "Johnnot" was Dominique You.

PIERRE LAFITTE'S CELL, CABILDO COURTYARD

COURTYARD AT 714 SAINT PETER STREET,
NEW ORLEANS

Pierre Goes to Jail

Before the news of the Grand Jury's action could be spread through the city, a platoon of dragoons was sent to scour the usual haunts of the Baratarians. Pierre Lafitte, caught off guard, was arrested in the street near the Place D'Armes. He was hustled off to the Calaboose and locked up in the strongest cell. Bail was denied.

Jean Lafitte hastened to New Orleans to confer with Sauvinet. This time he came secretly, and was not seen in public. But, for the first time, Sauvinet's money failed to procure the release of one of the Baratarians. The Custom Officials had seen to that. Jean and Pierre Lafitte had both eluded justice before; this time no chances would be taken.

Chapter XV

JEAN ACQUIRES A LAWYER AND A MISTRESS

WHEN John Randolph Grymes, the district attorney, returned home the next night a messenger was waiting to see him. The man must have been known to Mr. Grymes, for he accompanied him without question to a cottage near the ramparts of the city. Jean Lafitte was waiting there.

In gathering material for this book, I talked with a woman who told me a story of this meeting between John Grymes and Jean Lafitte. It is a fragment, handed down from mother to daughter, for four generations. I must withhold the name of the woman who told me, for reasons which will appear. Therefore I can only offer the tale to you as I heard it, to accept or reject as you see fit. Here it is:

Jean Acquires a Lawyer and a Mistress

The quadroon girl, Marie Louise Villars, was soon to bear a second child for Pierre Lafitte. When the news of his arrest reached her, she was overcome with fear and grief. Her mother and her sister Catherine did what they could to comfort her, but it was little enough.

Jean Lafitte came to their cottage late in the afternoon. He was very tired. The mother gave him supper, but he could not eat. There was a strong bond of affection between the brothers, and the love which Marie had for Pierre endeared her to Jean. On this night he was restless, roaming "like a wild beast" up and down in the candle-light, as he waited for the return of his messenger. He said nothing, and the women were silent too.

A knock on the door startled them all. Lafitte hid himself in Marie's bedroom while Catherine opened the door. Outside were Grymes and the messenger. Grymes came in, somewhat mystified, and the messenger waited at the gate, on guard. Lafitte came into the room, smiling, and he seemed to have forgotten his fatigue—or he was acting a part. He called for wine, and the mother served the men, and withdrew, closing the door.

The men remained in conversation for an hour or more, and although the women listened, they could hear nothing. Suddenly there was a noise "as though some one had struck the table with his open hand," and Grymes cried out, "By God, I'll do it!"

Soon Lafitte called for brandy, and the mother hastened in with the decanter and small glasses. Lafitte was standing beside the four-post bed, his dark head in strong relief against the white mosquito-*baire,* his eyes and teeth flashing. Grymes was lolling in an armchair beside the table, laughing immoderately. He said: "Livingston and I can get you out of hell, if necessary." The men sat for another hour, the bottle passing back and forth between them.

Marie Villars got out of bed in the adjoining room, and put on a trailing white gown trimmed with lace, "loose, so her condition would not be too apparent," and came to the men, begging for news. Grymes gave her a jaunty greeting (he had danced with her at the Quadroon Balls two years before) and assured her that he could secure freedom for Pierre Lafitte. "Leave it to me!" he said. Marie Villars kissed his hand, and he rebuked her for it, as "he was American and didn't like such things." He looked at the fifteen-year-old sister, Catherine, who stood silently by; and he commented on her luminous eyes and the flush in her cheeks; but he told her that she was too thin, and that she needed meat on her bones: "You should eat more gumbo, and get fat like your sister." The women smiled politely, but considered the remark in bad taste. Presently Grymes went away, and the messenger went with him, carrying a lantern.

Jean Lafitte had been all animation and gaiety when Grymes was present, but now he put his head down on the table and his shoulders shook. Catherine, the young girl, tried to comfort him. "He was like God to her, and

Jean Acquires a Lawyer and a Mistress

she loved him as a dog loves a man. Women of mixed blood are like that." She brought water in a bowl and towels, and wiped his face and hands. Unresisting, he sat there; nor did he drive her away with a laugh, as he did sometimes. The mother led Marie from the room.

The slim child knelt on the floor and unlaced the man's heavy boots. She undressed him as a mother would undress a baby; and he allowed her to do so. He sat staring into space, a man lost in some dark dream. The girl turned back the snowy sheets and he lay down; his rumpled hair was black against the pillow. Catherine kissed his forehead, sighed, and drew the curtains of mosquito netting around the bed. Then, with dragging feet, she went to the table and extinguished the candle.

She had reached the threshold when he spoke to her. It was only a word, but she answered with a glad cry. She turned and went back to him.

The quadroon mother softly closed the door between the rooms.

The story was told to me by a descendant of Marie Villars and Pierre Lafitte. The tragedy of mixed blood has embittered her. She lives obscurely among people who think of her as a white woman, and for this reason must remain anonymous. It was this woman who told me of the Lafitte records in the archives of the Saint Louis Cathedral. "You may look there," she said, "and see if I am telling the truth." Part of what I found has been told already; other records will be quoted in their proper places.

Oddly enough, she could not tell me what became of Catherine Villars, or "Jeannette" as she was called; but she gave me a clue.

Chapter XVI

JOHN GRYMES AND EDWARD LIVINGSTON

THERE was a sensation in New Orleans when John Randolph Grymes resigned from the office of District Attorney, and announced that he and Edward Livingston had undertaken the defense of the brothers Lafitte.

Grymes and Livingston were two of the most distinguished members of the Louisiana bar. They were both Americans, both had a wide following, both were friends of Governor Claiborne. Nevertheless, they had done this preposterous thing. Rumor said that each of them was to receive twenty thousand dollars as a fee. It was an enormous sum for those days.

Public opinion was divided. Some said that if Grymes and Livingston had undertaken to clear the Lafittes of

119

Lafitte the Pirate

the charges against them, there could be no truth in the belief that the Lafittes were guilty of piracy; others said cynically, that the lawyers had been bought outright, and that they had sold their birthright for the usual mess of pottage.

In open court, the District Attorney who had succeeded Grymes, charged him with having been "seduced out of the path of honor and duty by the blood-stained gold of pirates." Grymes promptly challenged him to a duel, shot him neatly through the hip, and crippled him for life.

It does appear, as one looks back across a century, that Claiborne's estimate of the Lafittes may have been somewhat harsh; for, although Grymes was a hail-fellow-well-met, and highly unconventional in his behavior and opinions, Edward Livingston was a conservative lawyer of long experience, a man of wide reputation, well-to-do, and highly regarded in the city. In 1814, Livingston was fifty years old, and even the sum of twenty thousand dollars should not have been too great a temptation. His career was so remarkable that I must leave the Lafittes for a moment and tell you about him.

Edward Livingston was born in New York State in 1764. He was a younger brother of Robert R. Livingston who played the memorable part in the purchase of Louisiana from France. Edward Livingston was graduated from Princeton, read law, practised in New York City, and was elected to Congress in 1795. In 1801 he was ap-

ORLEANS ALLEY, BESIDE THE CATHEDRAL

AN OLD INN, NEW ORLEANS

pointed by President Jefferson to the office of United States Attorney. Subsequently he was elected Mayor of New York City. In 1803, through the dishonesty of a clerk, he found himself a defaulter to the National Government. He resigned his position, sold all of his property in order to make good the shortage, and went to New Orleans to begin life over again. Immediately he came into prominence as an American lawyer in that Creole city. He framed a Code of Procedure for the Territory of Orleans which was used in Louisiana for many years. He was a leading figure in many famous legal cases, became important socially; and he was perhaps as well known a lawyer as one could find anywhere, when he announced the fact that he was to defend the Lafittes in conjunction with John Grymes.

But even these two famous ones could not procure the release of the prisoner. Midsummer came, and Pierre had been in the Calaboose for nearly two months. His trial was fast approaching and the lawyers made elaborate preparations for his defense, as well as for the defense of the unapprehended Jean. Jean Lafitte was in hiding. He appeared sometimes in New Orleans and was seen by this one and that, but he walked no more with easy nonchalance in the city's streets. He made trips about the State; and, as we have seen in Martha Martin's memoir, he was hiding in an inn at Donaldsonville in June.

The lawyers, after exhausting all other means, tried

Lafitte the Pirate

in August to secure Pierre's release on the plea that the confinement in jail, and the chains which weighed him down, were affecting his health. As in nearly every other incident of this period, we have only fragments of records upon which to rely for information. But this statement by two doctors, dated August 10th, 1814, is interesting in that it gives a glimpse of Pierre in jail. This paper is a part of the Pelletier collection:

In compliance with the direction of the Honorable Dominick A. Hall, judge of the District Court of the State of Louisiana, to examine into the state of health of Pierre Lafitte, confined in jail, and to report our opinion on the expediency of relieving him of his irons in his confinement, have forthwith to state:

That said Lafitte appears to have suffered about two years ago an apoplectic fit succeeded by palsy of the left side, and that he is habitually subject to paroxysms resembling hysteria.

We further report that said Lafitte is at present entirely free from any symptom indicating the probability of an early return of apoplexy; that the lowness of spirit from agitation of mind appears to be the only indisposition he labors under.

With due regard therefore to every indulgence of a prisoner, we are of opinion that there is no apparent necessity of relieving him of the irons, which have been applied as a means of security; and as far as may be consistent with safety, we would beg leave to recommend that he should be occasionally indulged in taking as much exercise as his confinement within the walls of the jail will admit of.

(Signed) Louis Heermann,   New Orleans,
                William Flood.   August 10th, 1814.

122

John Grymes and Edward Livingston

So Pierre Lafitte remained bound with heavy chains in the Calaboose through the long summer months. He was helpless, ill and embittered. The messages which came to him from his lawyers were unsatisfying enough, although he learned that his brother was conducting the affairs of Barataria with his customary efficiency and despatch. He learned, too, that the British had called no halt in their attack on the United States. . . . There had been fighting near Niagara Falls and at Lundy's Lane; and by August the news came that the principal American ports were blockaded by the enemy. At approximately the time that the doctors were refusing Pierre's request that his chains be struck off, the British forces were landing near Washington and were marching on the city. President Madison was forced to flee, leaving his dinner on the table; Dolly Madison was following in mad haste carrying the Declaration of Independence with her, presumably under her arm. The English forces fired the Capitol. Francis Scott Key watched the shelling of Fort Henry as he lay a prisoner in a British ship in the harbor at Baltimore, and dashed off "The Star-Spangled Banner." . . . English vessels appeared in the Gulf of Mexico; an invasion of Louisiana seemed almost inevitable.

And it was at this critical moment that Jean Lafitte met Governor Claiborne's wife.

Chapter XVII

THE GOVERNOR'S LADY

GRACE KING, one of the most charming of all chroniclers of the old New Orleans, tells an anecdote of Jean Lafitte's meeting with the Governor's wife. Miss King had it from a Creole lady, who in turn had it from her grandmother, and this quotation of a quotation is so amusing that I cannot resist quoting it once more.

Lafitte, so the story goes, was in the habit of stopping at the plantation home of a wealthy Creole family, when he passed by on his way from Barataria to New Orleans:

"I assure you he was a fascinating gentleman of fine appearance, and although described by the American as a pirate, he was really a privateer. . . . The fact that my grandmother received him as a friend, is a sufficient answer to any doubts as to his qualifications. . . . There was a price upon his head,

The Governor's Lady

and when he appeared at the plantation of my grandmother, she, with extreme agitation and anxiety told him . . . 'You must not go to the city. You must return at once after supper. Your life, I tell you it's your life that is in danger.' Lafitte laughed her fears to scorn. In the midst of her arguments and his gay expostulations, the servant announced another arrival, another guest. My grandmother turned her head, and at the instant was embraced by her most intimate friend, Mrs. Claiborne, the wife of the governor, the most beautiful of Creoles, the most coquettish, the most charming woman in the city. In great perplexity, but conquering nevertheless all traces of it, my grandmother, with quick presence of mind, introduced Monsieur Lafitte as Monsieur Clement, and then hurriedly went out of the room, leaving her guests together. She called Henriette, her confidential servant. 'Henriette,' she said, looking straight into the eyes of the devoted negress, 'Henriette, Governor Claiborne has put a price upon Monsieur Lafitte's head. Anyone who takes him prisoner and carries him to the governor will receive five hundred dollars, and M. Lafitte's head will be cut off. Send all the other servants away, all the children. Do you set the table and wait upon us yourself alone, and remember to call Monsieur Lafitte Monsieur Clement—Monsieur Clement, and be careful before Madame Claiborne.' The woman responded as was expected of her, and acted with perfect tact and discretion.

"The supper passed off brilliantly. The beautiful, fascinating woman instantaneously made an impression on the no less handsome and fascinating man, who never appeared bolder, more original, more sure of himself. The repartee was sparkling, the laughter continuous, the conversation full of *entrain*, and so pleasing to both as to render them oblivious of all my grandmother's efforts to put an end to the meal. And after

125

wards she could not separate the new acquaintances until late bedtime.

" 'My friend,' she then said to Lafitte, 'return, return immediately. Indeed, your life is in danger. Go where you can defend yourself.'

"Lafitte promised and took his leave, but it was always supposed that he spent the night on the plantation, held by the glamour of the presence of the wife of the governor, his great enemy.

"The next day, Madame Claiborne returned to the city, voluble in praise of the most remarkable man she had ever met."

[The rest of the story concerns Mrs. Claiborne's surprise when she found out who the charming gentleman was, but this—at the moment—does not concern us.]

The Governor's wife was not the only one who found Jean Lafitte a delightful companion. Old diners-out in New Orleans were fond of telling the story of the visit that John Randolph Grymes made to Barataria, and of the wonders he found there. They heard it from Grymes himself; it was his favorite after-dinner story.

Shortly after the two American lawyers undertook the case of the Lafittes, they were invited to come to Grande Terre and personally receive their fees—twenty thousand dollars apiece. Grymes was eager to go, for, as Grace King says, he was "an easy moralist and adventurous" and this type of bizarre experience was just the thing to delight him. But Livingston, older, more dignified and more conventional, refused the honor, but of-

The Governor's Lady

fered his colleague ten per cent commission to collect his share.

Although several historians speak of this visit to Barataria, no date is given; but it must have been sometime prior to September first, 1814. This seems somewhat odd, as Pierre Lafitte was still in jail; but it is possible that the money was paid as a retaining fee. But to Grande Terre went Grymes, and Lafitte received him royally.

In his old age, Grymes would tell the story, roaring with mirth as he spoke of the princely hospitality of the innocent, persecuted Baratarians. For a whole week, Jean Lafitte entertained him, and for a week, Grymes regarded the world through a rosy haze. "A fine fellow! Delicious food! Priceless linens and silver plate! And as for the wines and cordials—well!" Grymes would kiss the tips of his stubby fingers, then toss the kiss away.

"What a misnomer," the old man would exclaim, "to call the most polished gentleman in the world a pirate!" and he would shout with laughter.

At the end of the debauch, Lafitte accompanied him to the mouth of the Mississippi in a yawl, laden with boxes of Spanish gold and silver. There his host left him, and Grymes, with his personal body-guards, made the slow voyage up the river, stopping to visit many plantation owners on the way. He was entertained wherever he stopped, and the doubloons were exhibited to the wondering eyes of the planters. Nor could this gay gentleman resist the lure of the card-tables; and it is said that when he reached New Orleans, every penny of his fee had been gambled away.

This last incident, as Grymes told it, was the most amusing part of his story.

Chapter *XVIII*

THE BRITISH OFFER

SHORTLY after sunrise on September third, the Baratarians were startled by a cannon-shot from the Gulf. Before the rolling echoes of the detonation died away, shouting men were rushing from every direction down to the
beach. Grande Terre was like a disturbed ant-hill.

Lafitte ordered out a small boat with four oarsmen
and proceeded rapidly to the pass between the two islands.
Just beyond the inlet lay a brig-of-war with the British
flag at her masthead. As soon as Lafitte's boat came into
sight, a gig shot out from the side of the vessel and came
toward him. In this gig were three officers, two in naval
uniform and one in the scarlet of the British army. They
carried a white signal-flag in the bow and a British flag

in the stern of their boat. Lafitte was somewhat puzzled, and acted with his usual caution.

As the British gig approached the Baratarians, one of the officers called out his identity. He was Captain Lockyer, of his Majesty's navy, with a lieutenant of the same service, he said; and the officer in red was Captain McWilliams of the army. They were anxious to communicate with Mr. Lafitte as they had an important message for him. Was he among the islands?

Lafitte made himself known and invited them to come ashore.

From the description of the entertainment that followed, the presence of Mr. John Randolph Grymes seems the only thing lacking. The officers were received into the house where a lavish breakfast was served—a meal that lasted for hours on end. There were the finest wines of Spain and France, tropical fruits, game and many varieties of Gulf fish, all served upon the finest linen, and in dishes of heavy carved silver. Jean Lafitte was at his best. No, there must be no talk of business until after the meal was ended—in Louisiana such a thing was unheard of! The officers were astonished to find such grace and hospitality among the pirates, and it was not until midday, when they sat smoking the finest of Cuban cigars and sipping rare old brandy, that their host opened the packet of papers.

The first document proved to be a proclamation by Lieutenant-Colonel Edward Nicholls, commanding his

The British Offer

Britannic Majesty's forces in the Floridas. It was an appeal to Louisianians to join the English against the United States. It is so florid in style, and so remarkable in other ways, that I give it here in full:

Native of Louisiana! on you the first call is made to assist in liberating from a faithless imbecile government, your paternal soil: Spaniards, Frenchmen, Italians and British whether settled or residing for a time in Louisiana, on you also I call to aid me in this just cause: the American usurpation in this country must be abolished and the lawful owners of the soil put in possession. I am at the head of a large body of Indians, well armed, disciplined and commanded by British officers—a good train of artillery with every requisite, seconded by the powerful aid of a numerous British and Spanish squadron of ships and vessels of war. Be not alarmed, inhabitants of the country at our approach; the same good faith and disinterestedness which has distinguished the conduct of Britons in Europe, accompanies them here; you will have no fear of litigious taxes imposed on you for the purpose of carrying on an unnatural and unjust war; your property, your laws, the peace and tranquillity of your country, will be guaranteed to you by men who will suffer no infringement of theirs; rest assured that these brave red men only burn with an ardent desire of satisfaction for their wrongs they have suffered from the Americans, to join you in liberating these southern provinces from their yoke and drive them into those limits formerly prescribed by my sovereign. The Indians have pledged themselves in the most solemn manner not to injure in the slightest degree the persons or properties of any but enemies to their Spanish or English fathers; a flag over any door

Lafitte the Pirate

whether Spanish, French or British will be a certain protection, nor dare any Indian put his foot on the threshold thereof, under the penalty of death from his own countrymen; not even an enemy will an Indian put to death, except resisting in arms, and as for injuring helpless women and children, the red men by their good conduct and treatment to them (if it be possible) make the Americans blush for their more inhuman conduct lately on the Escambia, and within a neutral territory.

Inhabitants of Kentucky, you have too long borne with grievous impositions—the whole brunt of the war has fallen on your brave sons; be imposed on no longer, but either range yourselves under the standard of your forefathers, or observe a strict neutrality; if you comply with either of these offers, whatever provisions you send down will be paid for in dollars and the safety of the persons bringing it as well as the free navigation of the Mississippi guaranteed to you.

Men of Kentucky, let me call to your view (and I trust to your abhorrence) the conduct of those factions which hurried you into this civil, unjust and unnatural war at the time when Great Britain was straining every nerve in defence of her own and the liberties of the world—when the bravest of her sons were fighting and bleeding in so sacred a cause—when she was spending millions of her treasure in endeavouring to pull down one of the most formidable and dangerous tyrants that ever disgraced the form of man—when groaning Europe was almost in her last gasp—when Britons alone showed an undaunted front—basely did those assassins endeavour to stab her from the rear; she was turned on them renovated from the bloody but successful struggle—Europe is happy and free, and she now hastens justly to avenge the unprovoked insult. Show them that you are not collectively unjust; leave that contemptible few to shift for themselves, let those slaves of the tyrant

The British Offer

send an embassy to Elba, and implore his aid, but let every honest, upright American spurn them with united contempt. After the experience of twenty-one years, can you any longer support those brawlers for liberty who call it freedom when themselves are free; be no longer their dupes—accept of my offers—everything I have promised in this paper I guarantee to you on the sacred honour of a British officer.

Given under my hand at my head-quarters, Pensacola, this 29th day of August, 1814.

EDWARD NICHOLLS

Despite the high-flown language, it is stupid on face value; and Louisianians had experienced quite enough trouble with Indians to know something of their methods of warfare. The address to the men of Kentucky we may disregard; and the part concerning the promises made "on the sacred honour of a British officer" was only likely to stir the Creoles to mirth. All in all, it was exactly as the historian Gayarré sums it up—although whether he writes seriously or humorously, I have never decided: "This document," he says, "so faulty in style, and so deficient in common sense, produced no more effect on those to whom it was addressed than if it had forever remained locked up in the confused brains which gave it to the world."

Lafitte read it twice, and said nothing. Then he opened the second paper. This proved to be a letter addressed to "Mr. Lafitte, or commandant at Barataria." It bid frankly for the pirate's services in the British navy; and it promised rewards to him and to his men.

Lafitte the Pirate

Sir:

I have arrived in the Floridas for the purpose of annoying the only enemy Great Britain has in the world, as France and England are now friends. I call on you with your brave followers to enter into the service of Great Britain in which you shall have the rank of a Captain; lands will be given to you all in proportion to your respective ranks on a peace taking place, and I invite you on the following terms:

Your property shall be guaranteed to you and your persons protected; in return for which I ask you to cease all hostilities against Spain or the allies of Great Britain.—Your ships and vessels to be placed under the orders of the commanding officer on this station, until the commander-in-chief's pleasure is known, but I guarantee their fair value at all events. I herewith enclose you a copy of my proclamation to the inhabitants of Louisiana, which will, I trust point out to you the honourable intentions of my government. You may be an useful assistant to me, in forwarding them; therefore, if you determine, lose no time. The bearer of this, Captain M'Williams will satisfy you on any other point you may be anxious to learn as will Captain Lockyer of the Sophia, who brings him to you. We have a powerful re-enforcement on its way here, and I hope to cut out some other work for the Americans than oppressing the inhabitants of Louisiana. Be expeditious in your resolves and rely on the verity of

Your very humble servant,

EDWARD NICHOLLS

The leader of the Baratarians may have felt a desire to smile when he read this, thinking no doubt of the nu-

134

The British Offer

merous English and Spanish vessels he had taken as prizes, and of the surprise that would be felt in certain quarters if he accepted the offer and became an English captain. But still he said nothing, and opened the third letter. This proved to be a communication from the Hon. William Henry Percy, captain of His Majesty's ship *Hermes* and senior officer in the Gulf of Mexico, to Nicholas Lockyer, Esq., commander of H. M. Sloop *Sophia:*

Sir:

You are hereby required and directed after having received on board an officer belonging to the first battalion of Royal colonial marines to proceed, in His Majesty's sloop under your command, without a moment's loss of time for Barataria.

On your arrival at that place you will communicate with the chief persons there—you will urge them to throw themselves under the protection of Great Britain—and, should you find them inclined to pursue such a step, you will hold out to them that their property shall be secured to them, that they shall be considered British subjects and at the conclusion of the war, lands within his majesty's colonies in America will be allotted to them in return for these concessions. You will insist on an immediate cessation of hostilities against Spain, and in any case they should have any Spanish property not disposed of that it be restored and that they put their naval force into the hands of the senior officer here until the commander-in-chief's pleasure is known. In the event of their not being inclined to act offensively against the United States you will do all in your power to persuade them to a strict neutrality, and still endeavour to put a stop in their hostilities against Spain. Should you succeed completely in the object for which you are sent, you will concert such measures for the annoyance of the enemy as you judge best from circumstances; having an eye to the junction of their small armed vessels with me for the capture of Mobile, &c.

You will at all events yourself join me with the utmost despatch at this post with the accounts of your success.

Given under my hand on board his majesty's ship Hermes, at Pensacola, this 30th day of August, 1814.

W. H. Percy, Capt.

The fourth letter was dated two days later, and it carried a direct threat:

Having understood that some British merchantmen have been detained, taken into and sold by the inhabitants of Barataria, I have directed Captain Lockyer of his majesty's sloop Sophia to proceed to that place and inquire into the circumstances with positive orders to demand instant restitution, and in case of refusal to destroy to his utmost every vessel there as well as to carry destruction over the whole place and at the same time to assure him of the co-operation of all his majesty's naval forces on this station. I trust at the same time that the inhabitants of Barataria consulting their own interest, will not make it necessary to proceed to such extremities— I hold out at the same time a war instantly destructive to them; and on the other hand should they be inclined to assist Great Britain in her just and unprovoked war against the United States, the security of their property, the blessings of the British constitution—and should they be inclined to settle

The British Offer

on this continent, lands will at the conclusion of the war be allotted to them in his majesty's colonies in America. In return for all these concessions on the part of Great Britain, I expect that the directions of their armed vessels will be put into my hands (for which they will be remunerated), the instant cessation of hostilities against the Spanish government, and the restitution of any undisposed property of that nation.

Should any inhabitants be inclined to volunteer their services into his majesty's forces either naval or military for limited services, they will be received; and if any British subject being at Barataria wishes to return to his native country, he will, on joining his majesty's service, receive a free pardon.

Given under my hand on board H. M. ship Hermes, Pensacola, this 1st day of September, 1814.

W. H. PERCY, Captain and Senior Officer

Here indeed was a pretty problem. The threat was plain enough. Join us against your enemy, the United States, and help us defeat the Americans at New Orleans, and you will be safe. You will be rewarded as well. Refuse, and the British Navy will destroy Barataria.

Seeing that Lafitte hesitated, Captain McWilliams went on to supplement these written offers with verbal promises. He offered Lafitte the sum of thirty thousand dollars, and the rank of captain in the British navy. He assured the Baratarian that England and France were now fast friends, and that as a Frenchman, Lafitte's place was with the English. He pointed out that there was a reward offered for the pirate's capture, that his brother

137

was now languishing in jail, and that America was his natural enemy.

Still Lafitte listened politely, drank wine and said nothing.

Captain McWilliams, a little mellow with food and drink, went on to paint a glowing picture. Lafitte would be of great value as a guide through the bayous and rivers along the Louisiana coast; it was the purpose of the English Government to penetrate the upper country and act in concert with the forces in Canada; that everything was in readiness to carry on the war with increased vigor, and that success was sure, as little or no opposition was expected from the French and Spanish population of Louisiana. Finally Captain McWilliams laid his last card on the table. It was the English plan, he said, to free the slaves and arm them against the white people who resisted their authority and progress.

At last Lafitte spoke: "Your plan seems almost perfect," he said.

From his manner, Captain McWilliams was sure that the Baratarians would be his allies. And he consented gladly when Lafitte asked the English officers to excuse him for a few moments while he went to consult an old friend and associate in whom he had the greatest confidence.

But no sooner had Lafitte disappeared than Captain McWilliams was sorry that he had let him go. Outside the men were standing about on the beach. They had been

The British Offer

restless, and had murmured against the English. Lafitte had scarcely gone when a score of the men crowded into the room, crying out that the English were spies. The officers were roughly handled, and were hauled off to the guard-house and locked up. There were cries of "Kill the spies!" and "Turn them over to the Americans!"

But in the midst of the turmoil Lafitte returned, as suave as you please, and ordered his men to release the British gentlemen. How could they violate their leader's hospitality in such a fashion? The men did so, but stood in sullen groups, murmuring. Captain Lockyer, Captain McWilliams and the lieutenant were glad enough to be hustled down to the boat, and were willing enough to return in safety to their brig, carrying with them only the assurance that Lafitte would consider the matter carefully, talk it over with his officers, and let the English know his decision.

The delay seemed somewhat odd, but the Englishmen had no choice in the matter.

Chapter *XIX*

THE DOUBLE-DEALERS

Time! That was what Jean Lafitte needed now. He must think fast and he must think clearly. Everything depended on that.

Nobody can say what his thoughts were through that long September afternoon. There was no one to whom he could turn, and his decision must be made alone and at once. Some of those who have written of Lafitte think that he hesitated, and considered the British offer. I can find nothing in all the mass of fragmentary material examined which points to that. Nor do I doubt that his final conclusion could have been other than it was.

He was, first, a Louisianian; second, a Frenchman. His friends, his interests, his aims, all centered in the

The Double-Dealers

State. To a great number of men in the vicinity, he was a popular hero, a Robin Hood of the sea; and he was well aware of his popular following. He had no love for the English, nor for Spain; nor, for that matter, any great love for the United States laws, as typified by Governor Claiborne. Nevertheless, America was his country, and many of his followers were Americans. It is true that his brother was in jail, with the charge of piracy hanging over him; true, too, that piracy carried the penalty of hanging; and Jean Lafitte had a great affection for his brother who lay now in a dark cell with irons on his wrists and ankles.

However, John Grymes and Edward Livingston had assured Jean that it was nearly impossible to convict Pierre for piracy. The charge against Johnness, or Beluche, was for piracy on the *Santa,* a Spanish vessel, which was captured nine miles from Grande Isle and nine thousand dollars taken from her; the other charge was against Johnnot, or Dominique You, for capturing another Spanish vessel off Trinidad, and stealing her cargo, worth thirty thousand dollars. Pierre was charged as an accessory, before and after the fact, as one who did "upon land, to-wit: in the city of New Orleans, within the District of Louisiana, knowingly and willing aid, assist, procure, counsel and advise said piracies and robberies." Both Grymes and Livingston had pointed out that, if the matter came to trial at all, that the charge would be modified privateering, or violating the Neutral-

ity Laws of the United States, by bringing prizes *taken
from Spain* into the territory and selling them there.
Luckily, there was no evidence of such acts against an
American vessel.

The trial had not come up as yet. And if Jean Lafitte
sold out to the British, and if that treachery became
known, it was possible that summary justice might be
meted out to Pierre, helpless and in jail. That was not
pleasant to think about.

Another thing. Lafitte's men were largely American
in their sympathies; England was their enemy. They had
scuttled English ships, and they had fear, but no love for
that country. Nor would they have believed the English
promises. It is doubtful if half of them would have followed even Jean Lafitte against the United States.

There was still another thing. The extremely doubtful thirty thousand dollars, which the British had offered,
meant little to Lafitte. He had plenty of money; the merchandise alone that was stored in the warehouses at
Grande Terre was worth more than five hundred thousand dollars. And Lafitte's present position at the head of
his men was surely more important—and infinitely more
dramatic—than any captaincy in the British army or
navy.

And there was yet another troublesome thought.
Claiborne had just secured aid from the Federal Government; there were American warships in the New Orleans
harbor. For the first time, an available force was at hand

The Double-Dealers

and could be sent against Barataria. Suppose Lafitte sold out to the British? What was to prevent Claiborne's sending an attack against Grande Terre before he could get aid from the enemy?

Those were some of the things which Lafitte may have considered that golden September afternoon as he sat on the veranda of the house at Grande Terre. But aside from these things, I do not believe that, even for a moment, he wavered in his allegiance to Louisiana.

Moreover, I believe that a whispered word from him had stirred his men against the British and had forced their hurried leave. That sort of quick thinking would have been characteristic of the man; and it seems to me that his subsequent behavior proves conclusively that he would have never accepted the British offer.

But, Jean Lafitte did not fail to realize that this was an opportunity for him. More, he realized that his position was dramatic, heroic. And he determined to make the most of it. His love for drama was so ingrained that it was impossible for him to write a letter without "making phrases," as the Creoles called it. This gift, or weakness, as you prefer, is plainly apparent in the two letters which he wrote early in the morning of September fourth. The first was to John Blanque, a friend of his who was in the State Legislature. The second letter was to Governor Claiborne, and was inclosed in that of Blanque's. These letters are worth noting, for they reveal much. Here is the letter to Blanque:

143

Lafitte the Pirate

Sir,

Though proscribed by my adopted country, I will never let slip any occasion of serving her or of proving that she has never ceased to be dear to me. Of this you will here see a convincing proof. Yesterday, the 3rd of September, there appeared here, under a flag of truce, a boat coming from an English brig, at anchor about two leagues from the pass. Mr. Nicholas Lockyer, a British officer of high rank, delivered me the following papers; two directed to me, a proclamation, and the admiral's instructions to that officer, all herewith enclosed. You will see from their contents the advantages I might have derived from that kind of association.

I may have evaded the payment of duties to the custom house; but I have never ceased to be a good citizen; and all the offences I have committed I was forced to by certain vices in our laws. In short, sir, I make you the depository of the secret on which perhaps depends the tranquility of our country; please to make such use of it as your judgment may direct. I might expatiate on this proof of patriotism but I let the fact speak for itself.

I presume, however, to hope that such proceedings may obtain amelioration of the situation of my unhappy brother, with which view I recommend him particularly to your influence. It is in the bosom of a just man, of a true American, endowed with all other qualities that are honoured in society, that I think I am depositing the interests of our common country and that particularly concerns myself.

Our enemies have endeavored to work on me by a motive which few men would have resisted. They represented to me a brother in irons, a brother who is to me very dear; whose deliverer I might become, and I declined the proposal. Well

The Double-Dealers

persuaded of his innocence, I am free from apprehension as the issue of a trial, but he is sick and not in a place where he can receive the assistance his state requires. I recommend him to you, in the name of humanity.

As to the flag of truce, I have done with regard to it everything that prudence suggested to me at the time. I have asked fifteen days to determine, assigning such plausible pretexts, that I hope the term will be granted. I am waiting for the British officer's answer, and for yours to this. Be so good as to assist me with your judicious counsel in so weighty an affair.

I have the honour to salute you,

J. Lafitte

Some of the phrases that he "made" are extraordinary: "I have never ceased to be a good citizen; and all the offences I have committed I was forced to by certain vices in our laws!" And again: "Our enemies have endeavored to work on me by a motive which few men would have resisted!" And, at the end, how cleverly he tells of his double-dealing with the British.

In the letter to Claiborne he stated very distinctly his position, and his desires:

Sir,

In the firm persuasion that the choice made of you to fill the office of first magistrate of this state was dictated by the esteem of your fellow-citizens and was conferred on merit, I confidently address you on an affair on which may depend the safety of this country.

I offer to you to restore to this state several citizens who perhaps, in your eyes have lost that sacred title. I offer you

Lafitte the Pirate

them, however, such as you could wish to find them, ready to exert their utmost efforts in defence of the country. This point of Louisiana, which I occupy, is of great importance in the present crisis. I tender my services to defend it; and the only reward I ask is that a stop be put to the proscription against me and my adherents, by an act of oblivion for all that has been done hitherto. I am the stray sheep, wishing to return to the sheepfold. If you were thoroughly acquainted with the nature of my offences, I should appear to you much less guilty, and still worthy to discharge the duties of a good citizen. I have never sailed under any flag but that of the republic of Carthagena, and my vessels are perfectly regular in that respect. If I could have brought my lawful prizes into the ports of this state, I should not have employed the illicit means that have caused me to be proscribed. I decline saying more on the subject until I have the honour of your excellency's answer, which I am persuaded can be dictated only by wisdom. Should your answer not be favorable to my ardent desires, I declare to you that I will instantly leave the country, to avoid the imputation of having co-operated towards an invasion on this point, which cannot fail to take place, and to rest secure in the acquittal of my own conscience.

I have the honour to be
Your excellency's, &c.

J. Lafitte

Note that phrase: "I am the stray sheep, wishing to return to the sheepfold." It is probable that he smacked his lips when he wrote that. And notice how definite he is (for once) in this: "The only reward I ask is that a stop be put to the proscription against me and my adherents," in other words: "Let me alone, and I'll help you." And,

The Double-Dealers

at the end he makes the gesture magnificent: he will leave, depart, decamp, rather than have the slightest suspicion fall upon him of giving aid to the enemy.

Do not mistake me: I believe that he was perfectly sincere; but I also believe that he could no more help making a play to the gallery than he could help breathing; or perhaps it would be better to say that this type of heroics was the breath of life to him.

He sealed the two letters together, and inclosed with them the entire British correspondence, including the proclamation; and he sent the packet by messenger in a fast pirogue through the bayous to the city. Twelve hours later Blanque received them.

As soon as the man had gone, Lafitte sat down to write a letter to Captain Lockyer. Fortunately for us the letter is still extant, and it is as pretty a piece of duplicity as one could find in a long day's journey. Note well; and note especially the delicate bit of flattery at the end:

Sir,

The confusion which prevailed in our camp yesterday and this morning, and of which you have a complete knowledge, has prevented me from answering in a precise manner to the object of your mission; nor even at this moment can I give you all the satisfaction that you desire; however, if you could grant me a fortnight, I would be entirely at your disposal at the end of that time—this delay is indispensable to send away three persons who have alone occasioned all the disturbance—the two who were the most troublesome are to leave this place in eight days, and the other is to go to town—the remainder of the time is necessary to enable me to put my affairs in order.— You may communicate with me, in sending a boat to the eastern point of the pass, where I will be found. You have inspired me with more confidence than the admiral, your superior officer, could have done himself; with you alone I wish to deal, and from you also I will claim, in due time, the reward of the service which I may render to you.

Be so good, sir, as to favour me with an answer, and believe me yours, &c.

J. LAFITTE

The contents of the packet which was delivered to Representative Blanque caused immediate consternation in official circles in New Orleans, already apprehensive of a sudden invasion by the English.

Blanque went straight to Claiborne, and the Governor quickly summoned his naval and military advisers to consider the matter. In the committee were Major-General Jacques Villere, Commodore Patterson of the United States navy, and Colonel Ross of the regular army. The Governor asked two questions: First, whether the letters were genuine? Second, whether it was proper that the Governor should hold any intercourse or enter into any correspondence with Lafitte or his associates? The committee answered no to both questions.

That is, both Patterson and Ross voted no. Villere voted a vehement yes. Claiborne, presiding, had no vote, although it is easy to surmise in which direction his influence went.

The Double-Dealers

Villere said that he believed the letters were genuine, and that Lafitte and his men were needed in case of invasion; but he was outvoted.

Collector Dubourg, in charge of the customs for the Government in New Orleans, was particularly insistent that this pirates' stronghold, or smugglers' retreat, be done away with at once. And the more law-abiding merchants of the city were equally insistent that the State assist the Government as it was sworn to do.

So Lafitte's offer was disregarded, but no direct answer was given. Claiborne, like Lafitte, was not averse to a little double-dealing.

Patterson and Ross were anxious to attack the stronghold at Barataria at once. . . . There were rich prizes to be had there.

How John Blanque felt is not stated, and it is likely that he did not know the outcome of the committee meeting. But somebody was active in another quarter that day. What happened I cannot tell you, but the next morning, the New Orleans newspapers carried the following advertisement:

$1,000 REWARD

Will be paid for the apprehension of PIERRE LAFITTE, who broke and escaped last night from the prison of the parish. Said PIERRE LAFITTE is about five feet ten inches in height, stout made, light complexion, and somewhat cross-eyed; further description is considered unnecessary, as he is very well known in the city.

Said LAFITTE took with him three negroes. The above reward will be paid to any person delivering the said LAFITTE to the subscriber.

J. H. HOLLAND,
Keeper of the Prison.

While Pierre was making the trip through the bayous to Grande Terre, Jean intercepted another letter which contained a warning of the intentions of the British toward New Orleans. He promptly despatched it to Blanque, along with this letter of his own:

Grande Terre, 7th. September, 1814

Sir,

You will always find me eager to evince my devotedness to the good of the country, of which I endeavored to give some proof in my letter of the 4th, which I make no doubt you received. Amongst other papers that have fallen into my hands, I send you a scrap which appears to me of sufficient importance to merit your attention.

Since the departure of the officer who came with the flag of truce, his ship, with two other ships of war, have remained on the coast, within sight. Doubtless this point is considered as important. We have hitherto kept on a respectable defensive; if, however, the British attach to the possession of this place the importance they give us room to suspect they do, they may employ means above our strength. I know not whether, in that case, proposals of intelligence with government would be out

The Double-Dealers

of season. It is always from my high opinion of your enlightened mind, that I request you to advise me in this affair.

I have the honour to salute you,

J. LAFITTE

Three days later, Pierre wrote again to Blanque; both brothers were now tense with excitement, and were worried because they had received no replies to their communications:

Grande Terre, 10th September, 1814

Sir,

On my arrival here I was informed of all the occurrences that have taken place; I think I may justly commend my brother's conduct under such difficult circumstances. I am persuaded he could not have made a better choice than in making you the depositary of the papers that were sent to us and which may be of great importance to the state. Being fully determined to follow the plan that may reconcile us with the government, I herewith send you a letter directed to his excellency the governor, which I submit to your discretion, to deliver or not, as you may think proper. I have not yet been honored with an answer from you. The moments are precious; pray send me an answer that may serve to direct my measures in the circumstances in which I find myself.

I have the honour to be, &c.

P. LAFITTE

Both men were very much in earnest, and the days must have seemed long indeed as they waited; but no answer came.

Lafitte the Pirate

The only apparent result of the Lafittes' warning was to hasten the attack on Barataria by Colonel Ross and Commodore Patterson.

In the meantime, the fortnight asked for by Jean Lafitte had passed, and the British were impatient. Captain Lockyer's vessel appeared off Grande Terre, and remained in the inlet for several days. At last, his patience worn out, he sailed away.

Chapter XX

BARATARIA IS DESTROYED

On the day that Governor Claiborne's committee decided to hold no correspondence with Jean Lafitte, Commodore Patterson began assembling his forces for an attack on Barataria.

By September eleventh he was ready; and at that dark hour which precedes the dawn (always a pleasant time for optimists), three barges loaded with armed men and ammunition left the New Orleans levee and drifted down with the river's current. At Balize, a village near the mouth of the Mississippi, they were joined by Colonel Ross and his fleet of six gunboats and the schooner *Carolina*. It was a strong force and more than a match for the strength of Lafitte's men.

The fleet went slowly along the Gulf Coast, among

Lafitte the Pirate

the small islands, until Grande Terre and Grand Isle were in sight. This was the early morning of September 16th.

Because of the direction from which they came—from the Gulf—there was some doubt among the Baratarians as to the identity of the vessels: it was thought at first that this might be the British brigs-of-war returning to demand Lafitte's answer.

When the fleet was sighted, the Baratarians made preparations for resistance, arming themselves and collecting on the beach. Their cannon were placed in position, their matches lighted, when, to their dismay, they saw the American flag fluttering in the fog.

There was immediate consternation; not one of them was willing to fire on that flag. Instead the men scattered in every direction, abandoning everything. Eighty of them were captured; many hundreds escaped into the marshes. The Lafittes were not among the captives, but Dominique You was taken. The soldiers, under the command of Ross and Patterson broke open the storehouse and took possession of the rich merchandise which lay there. Their prize, or loot, if you prefer, was valued at more than five hundred thousand dollars.

Evidently the capture and destruction of Barataria took several days. On September 19th Colonel Ross wrote a hurried note to Major Reynolds and sent it back to New Orleans by messenger. He seems excited, and somewhat vague; and the letter appears to have been written in the midst of the mêlée:

Barataria is Destroyed

I have just time to say that in addition to taking some of the ringleaders, we are in possession of all the flotilla except a schooner that was burnt to the water's edge. There were here, say seven fine schooners outside of the island. One of 150 tons armed complete. Captain Henley lay off the bar and out-manoeuvered her; she ran for us, getting between two fires. Signal—A gun from the commodore; another strange sail in sight.

Lafitte's force consisted of thirteen vessels, and was composed of brigantines, polaccas and small schooners, two or three gunboats and feluccas, as well as many small boats. Some of these vessels and small boats escaped into the bayous where they were safe from pursuit.

The Louisiana Gazette on September 22nd, carried a copy of this letter from John K. Smith to the Honorable William Jones, Secretary of the Navy:

Sir—Captain Patterson left this place on the 11th inst. with three barges, and was joined at the Balize by six gun boats and the schooner *Carolina,* from whence he proceeded against Barataria. He has been completely successful in breaking up the nest of pirates at that place, and has taken nine vessels, some specie and a quantity of dry goods. The principal (Lafitte) escaped; but the second in command, Dominique, is taken. The number of prisoners taken is not known, nor are any of the particulars. A letter from that place states that Capt. Patterson would leave there on the 20th. He will therefore, no doubt, have the honor of giving you the result by the next mail.

The breaking up of this piratical establishment is of great

Lafitte the Pirate

importance to this country, it is ascertained that vessels clearing out from this port with passengers have been captured and every soul on board murdered; they took indiscriminately vessels of every nation, and the fact was perfectly known at Pensacola. The commanding British officer at the place recently made a communication in writing to Lafitte requesting his aid in an attack upon New Orleans, which was refused. That correspondence which is in the hands of Governor Claiborne no doubt has been communicated to the government.

In the gallant defence of Mobile Point the only two 24 pounders were injured and rendered useless—General Jackson has since made a requisition upon Captain Patterson for others to replace them, which have in his absence been furnished. I have the honor to be, etc.

J. K. SMITH,

Hon. William Jones, Secretary of the Navy.

Commodore Patterson's official report is dated October 10th, 1814, and was written in New Orleans. It says:

The force of the pirates was twenty pieces of cannon and from eight hundred to one thousand men of all nations and colours. I have brought with me six fine schooners, and one felucca, cruisers, and prizes of the pirates, and one armed schooner under Carthagenian colours, found in company and ready to oppose the force under my command.

In a second report to the Secretary of the Navy he says:

AT BARATARIA

A SPANISH VILLA ON BAYOU ST. JOHN

Barataria is Destroyed

On the 16th of September I made Barataria; some of the vessels showed Carthagenian colours; the pirates formed their vessels for battle near the entrance of the harbour. At half-past ten A.M. I perceived several smokes along the shore as signals, and at the same time, a white flag hoisted at the fore on board the schooner "The Lady of the Gulf," an American flag at the main, and a Carthagenian flag, under which the pirates cruise, at her topping lift. . . . The pirates had fired two of their schooners. I hauled down my white flag and made signal for battle, hoisting with it a large white flag bearing the words "Pardon to Deserters," having heard that there were a number of such from the United States Army and Navy there, who wished to return, if assured of pardon, and which the President's pardon offered until the 17th of September. . . . I perceived that the pirates were abandoning their vessels and were flying in all directions. I sent in pursuit of them. At meridian I took possession of all their vessels in the harbour, consisting of six schooners and one felucca, cruisers and prizes of the pirates, one brig, a prize, and two armed schooners under the Carthagenian flag, both in the line of battle with the armed vessels of the pirates, and apparently with the intention to aid them; their crews were at quarters, tompions out of their guns, and their matches lighted. . . . Colonel Ross landed and took possession of their establishment on shore, which consisted of forty houses of different sizes, badly constructed, and thatched with palmetto leaves. I have captured all their vessels in port, dispersed their band, without one of my brave fellows being hurt. . . .

On October 25th, Governor Claiborne wrote to James Monroe:

157

Lafitte the Pirate

You will have heard of the fortunate result of a joint attack by land and water under the orders of Colonel Ross of the 44 United States Regiment, and Captain Patterson of the Navy, against the Pirates and Smugglers of Barataria. . . . Of the meritorious conduct of Captain Patterson on that occasion I have borne testimony in a letter to the Secretary of the Navy, and I now, Sir, take the liberty to express to you my approbation of the zeal and activity displayed by Colonel Ross. It was at my particular request, that the Colonel detailed for the service, a detachment from his Regiment, and in commanding it in person, he gave additional proof of the patriotic feeling by which he was influenced. These pirates are at present dispersed, but to prevent their re-assembling, a naval force on this station, in peace or in war, will be indispensable.

Claiborne wrote also to General Andrew Jackson to tell him of the success of the expedition and the seizure of "the ill-begotten treasures of the pirates," as he called them.

Historians were not so well pleased as Governor Claiborne was:

"As for Lafitte and his companions," says Gayarré, the attitude of hostility which they had taken toward the British, the valuable information which they had imparted to Claiborne, and the offer of their services, do not seem to have softened his disposition toward them, or changed his views of their demerits."

Alexander Walker, whose history of "Jackson and New Orleans" is a standard work on the subject, goes further: "This was truly an ungrateful return for ser-

Barataria is Destroyed

vices which may now be justly estimated," Judge Walker writes. "Nor is it satisfactorily shown that mercenary motives did not mingle with those which prompted some of the parties engaged in that expedition."

It is true that Patterson and Ross claimed the five hundred thousand dollars worth of goods and merchandise, as well as the captured ships, as "lawful prizes." Perhaps that was fair enough; and surely it was not more than the Lafittes themselves had done. Or at least Governor Claiborne felt that way, and so expressed himself in a letter to John Grymes.

When Lafitte's letters, documents and his offer of service were forwarded to General Jackson, then at Mobile, he rejected them with scorn, having already by proclamation denounced the British for their overtures to "robbers, pirates, and hellish banditti."

And in New Orleans, a sinister story was passing from lip to lip. An inventory had been taken of the merchandise found in the storehouse at Grande Terre; among the booty was some jewelry, and linen, definitely identified as the property of a Creole lady who had sailed from New Orleans some time before, and had never been heard of afterwards.

The implication was all too plain. Men who had defended the Lafittes up to this time, were now in doubt. Others shook their heads; "And so they were pirates, after all."

The outlook was dark for the brothers Lafitte.

Chapter XXI

GENERAL ANDREW JACKSON

COLD weather came early that year. September's gold faded into gray and chill October. Rain poured down, and the city's streets became a sea of mud. It was almost as though the rain had fallen upon the hearts of the Creoles, too, for the people were full of foreboding.

New Orleans has always possessed that quality of quick laughter or fear: security and fine weather cause immediate joy, but storms or disasters sweep down with equal suddenness, bringing the population of the city from merriment to tragedy in one short day.

From the windows of the Claiborne house in Toulouse Street, the governor's wife looked petulantly at the pattering rain, then turned to examine again her silks and laces which filled the large *armoires* of mahogany and rose-wood; the handsome gowns were all useless now, and would remain useless until the rain ceased, for it was impossible to go out into a morass of mud and water. In the large room with fan light windows which overlooked the courtyard, the Governor continued to write his letters and despatches; he was making every attempt possible to bring help to New Orleans, and to stir the apathetic people to a realization of the danger before them. Each day brought rumors or news of British activity in the Mexican Gulf. More and more enemy vessels were arriving, and New Orleans was a city almost without defense. The poorly equipped troops which drilled nowadays in the slanting rain, were no match for the seasoned men of the British army. And from the news which came to Claiborne, he knew that the enemy would outnumber the Americans three to one.

Over at Tremoulet's Coffee House, Edward Livingston read resolutions to a "numerous and respectable" gathering of citizens in which allegiance to the United States was declared; and those who signed, promised to "repel with indignation every attempt to create disaffection and weaken the force of the country by exciting dissensions and jealousies at a moment when union is most necessary." A committee was named to coöperate with the constituted civil and military authorities in suggesting means of defense, and to repel invasion and preserve domestic tranquillity.

Lafitte the Pirate

The names of the committee are worth noting. The nine were: Edward Livingston, Pierre Foucher, Dussau de LaCroix, B. Morgan, G. M. Ogden, D. Bouligny, J. N. Destrehan, John Blanque, and A. McCarty. These men were as well known as any men in the city, and the fact that they were chosen for this important work shows that they were held in high regard by their fellow citizens. And yet . . . Jean Lafitte's two great friends were among them. John Blanque and Edward Livingston, one a Creole, the other an American.

Jean and Pierre Lafitte, John Grymes and Edward Livingston had held several secret meetings since the destruction of Barataria. The cottage near the ramparts served its purpose well, and behind those tight-barred doors, the conferences had been held. The four men had decided that there was only one thing to do; they must wait. Grymes and Livingston were strong in their belief that all would yet be well. They had prepared a suit against the United States for the recovery of property confiscated at Grande Terre, but, as both lawyers said, the time was inopportune. A battle was impending, and if Louisiana was taken by the British, any suit would be useless—they would be lucky enough to escape with their lives. But, if the Baratarians and the United States authorities could reach some agreement there was a possibility that the Lafittes could get their treasure back again.

In spite of all that had happened, Jean and Pierre

General Andrew Jackson

Lafitte were still anxious to join forces with the Americans against the British invasion. True, their offer had been rejected, but both Grymes and Livingston were confident that, in the end, the Baratarian forces would be accepted. They had good reason for such belief, too, for the American army was pitifully inadequate, and reinforcements did not appear to be forthcoming. "Wait until General Jackson comes," they said.

Grymes and Livingston brought news to the Lafittes from Dominique You and those other hapless Baratarians who were crowded into the dark cells of the Calaboose. These men would do whatever their leader told them to do—if Lafitte could secure their freedom.

Hundreds of men from Grande Terre and Grande Isle, who had escaped into the marshes at the time of the attack, were now gathered at Last Island—a large, low-lying body of land at the mouth of Bayou Lafourche, sixty miles west from "The Temple." Here they were safe from attack; and they promptly built their palmetto shelters and rigged out their small boats as before. As yet they did not dare return to Grande Terre, as officers of the United States were stationed there, owing to the importance of the waterway which led directly from the Mexican Gulf to the very door of New Orleans. Claiborne was afraid of an invasion from that direction, as testified by many references to Barataria in his letters to Andrew Jackson.

Jean Lafitte was in close touch with his men at Last

Lafitte the Pirate

Island—or Isle Dernière as it was called; and they, like the Baratarians in the Calaboose, were ready to obey his commands.

On the 30th of October, Claiborne wrote a rather curious letter to Rush, the Attorney-General of the United States at Washington. It is worth quoting, as it shows that the governor is not so violently opposed to the Baratarians as his previous letters lead us to believe. Or, it is possible that Livingston and Grymes had influenced him, and had caused him to alter his point of view. It is also possible that Claiborne, now having gained his ends in crushing Lafitte, felt that he could afford to be generous.

You have no doubt heard that the late expedition to Barataria had eventuated in the entire dispersion of the pirates and smugglers, and the capture of nearly all their cruisers [Claiborne wrote]. It is greatly to be regretted that neither the General nor State Government had not sooner been enabled to put down these banditti. The length of time they were permitted to continue their evil practices added much to their strength, and led the people here to view their course as less vicious. Measures tending to the prevention of crimes can alone relieve us from the distress of punishing them. . . . I have been at great pains to convince the people of this State that smuggling was a moral offence, but in this I have only partially succeeded. There are individuals here who, in every other respect, fulfill with exemplary integrity all the duties devolving upon them as fathers of families and citizens; but as regards smuggling, although they may not be personally concerned, they

General Andrew Jackson

attach no censure to those who are. It is the influence of education, habit, and bad example. . . . Occasionally, in conversation with ladies, I have denounced smuggling as dishonest, and very generally a reply, in substance as follows, would be returned: *That is impossible, for my grandfather, or my father, or my husband was, under the Spanish Government, a great smuggler, and he was always esteemed an honest man.* . . . Prosecutions are now pending in the District Court against several of the Baratarian offenders, and, in the course of the investigation it is probable the number implicated will be very considerable. Justice demands that the most culpable be punished with severity. But I see no good end to be attained by making the penalties of the law fall extensively and heavily. Should the President think proper to instruct the Attorney for District of Louisiana to select a few of the most hardened offenders of Barataria for trial, and to forbear to prosecute all others concerned, I think such an act of clemency would be well received . . . and attended with the best effects. A sympathy for these offenders is certainly felt by many of the Louisianians.

Claiborne called upon the Legislature to convene, in order to secure their aid in arming Louisiana against invasion. On the 14th of November he laid before the assembly a letter from General Jackson which gave proof that danger was close at hand: "Recent information from the most correct sources," wrote General Jackson to Claiborne, "has been received of an expedition of twelve or fifteen thousand men, sailing from Ireland early in September last, intended to attempt the conquest of Louisiana. You will therefore see the necessity of preparing for service, at an hour's notice, the whole body of the Louisiana

165

militia. I rely on your patriotism and activity, and hope not to be disappointed."

Claiborne was afraid of the Legislature. He was aware of their apathy, and he wrote to Jackson: "The Legislature have not as yet done anything to damp the public ardor. But I hope this body will be justly impressed with the dangers to which we are exposed, and will second all my efforts. But I fear, I much fear, they will not act with the promptitude and the energy which the crisis demands." Certainly this is a pessimistic document, but Claiborne had been Governor since 1803, and was in a position to know his constituents. The next day we find him writing to Governor Blount of Tennessee in the same strain: "But," he adds, "we shall, in any event, be made secure by those brave and determined men who are hastening from Tennessee and Kentucky. I await their arrival with much anxiety."

General Jackson reached New Orleans on the morning of December second. He rode on horseback from Mobile, accompanied by only half-a-dozen of his officers. He was a tall, gaunt man, restless, full of feverish energy. His iron-gray hair was long, and was drawn back from his sallow and hawk-like face; he was jaundiced, emaciated. He had been ill, and was then far from well. He had just completed one hard campaign and was facing another which seemed doomed to disaster. Nevertheless, he was there, and he was ready to save New Orleans or die in the attempt. He had written Claiborne to that end—and

General Andrew Jackson

any one who knew him, knew that his words were not an empty boast.

J. Kilty Smith, one of the leading American merchants of New Orleans, had some slight acquaintance with Jackson, and accordingly, rode out along the highway to meet him, shortly after sunrise. Smith was astonished to see the change which had taken place in the man in the year that had intervened since their last meeting. Jackson was a sick man; there could be no question about it.

The general was glad enough to stop at the merchant's house for breakfast, and to stretch his tired legs before an open fire. He lay back in an arm-chair in a moment's peaceful contentment, noting with tired eyes the spotless linen and silver dishes shining in the firelight.

Smith was a man of luxurious tastes: he had taken an old Spanish villa on Bayou St. John for his bachelor quarters, and had furnished it magnificently. A Creole lady who lived nearby had come over at Smith's request to supervise the breakfast, but when she saw Jackson sprawled before the fire, she was astonished. She stood in the doorway for a moment, looking at his threadbare clothes, his leather cap, and his blue Spanish cloak which was spattered with dried mud. She sighed as she looked down at his high dragoon boots which were so sadly in need of blacking. Then she called Smith from the room.

"Ah, Mr. Smith, how could you play such a trick upon me? You asked me to get your house ready to receive a great general. I did so, and almost worked myself to death to make your house *comme il faut*. And now I find that all my labor is thrown away on an ugly old Kentucky flatboatman! Where is your grand general, with his plumes, his long sword and his big mustache?"

Later that day General Jackson met Governor Claiborne, Commodore Patterson, Edward Livingston, John Grymes and Nicholas Girod, mayor of New Orleans. They were scarcely less astonished than the Creole lady had been when they observed Jackson's shabby appearance, but their surprise did not make them any less glad to see him. Much fine talk was exchanged, but almost immediately a difficulty presented itself. Nicholas Girod spoke only French, and Livingston had to act as an interpreter. Through the interpreter, Jackson assured the mayor that he had come to protect the city to the best of his ability; that he would drive the English from the shores of Louisiana or perish in the attempt, and he urged Girod to beg the people of New Orleans to forget all personal differences of opinion and join him against the British invasion. . . . Then he went to headquarters which had been arranged for him in Royal Street.

General Jackson had arrived. The news spread through the city, and New Orleans, the volatile, became immediately reassured. Everything would be safe now. Jackson would soon drive the British away.

And the general's behavior was indeed calculated to inspire confidence. He went to work without wasting an hour. The official reception over, he began to take stock of the possible defense of the city. He rode on horseback to the camps to inspect the troops. Some of these were volunteer organizations and consisted of merchants, lawyers, sons of planters, clerks and other well-to-do persons, well-equipped and a little proud of their appearance and discipline. Here Jackson showed himself a master of diplomacy, oddly at variance with his straight-forward exterior. He spoke a word of praise here, offered a suggestion there, and assured the officers that he appreciated their efforts. As a result, he became immediately popular with the troops.

Edward Livingston was appointed Jackson's military secretary. And promptly Mrs. Livingston gave a dinner for the general, where he appeared in full uniform and quite captivated the Creole ladies with his charm of manner. In Livingston's letters we find this:

To my astonishment this uniform was new, spotlessly clean and fitted his tall, slender form perfectly. I had seen him before only in the worn and careless fatigue uniform he wore on duty at headquarters. I had to confess to myself that the new and perfectly fitting uniform made almost another man of him.

I also observed that he had two sets of manners: One for the headquarters, where he dealt with men and the problems of war; the other for the drawing room, where he met the gentler sex and was bound by the etiquette of fair society. But he was equally at home in either. When we reached the middle of the room all the ladies rose. I said: "Madame and

Lafitte the Pirate

Mesdemoiselles, I have the honor to present Major-General Jackson of the United States Army."

The General bowed to Madame, and then right and left to the young ladies about her. Madame advanced to meet him, took his hand and then presented him to the young ladies severally, name by name. Unfortunately, of the twelve or more young ladies present—all of whom happened to be French—not more than three could speak English: and as the General understood not a word of French—except perhaps *Sacre bleu*—general conversation was restricted.

However, we at once sought the table, where we placed the General between Madame Livingston and Mlle. Eliza Chotard, an excellent English scholar, and with their assistance as interpreters, he kept up a lively all-around chat with the entire company. Of our wines he seemed to fancy most a fine old Madeira and remarked that he had not tasted anything like it since Burr's dinner at Philadelphia in 1797 when he (Jackson) was a senator. I well remembered that occasion, having been then a member of Congress from New York, and one of Burr's guests.

"So you have known Mr. Livingston a very long time," exclaimed Mlle. Chotard.

"Oh yes, Miss Chotard," he replied. "I had the honor to know Mr. Livingston probably before the world was blessed by your existence."

This was only one of a perfect fusillade of quick and apt compliments he bestowed with charming impartiality upon the pretty guests.

When the general had gone, the ladies no longer restrained their enthusiasm. "Is this your savage Indian-fighter? Is this your rough frontier general? Shame on you Mr. Livingston to deceive us so! He is a veritable *preux chevalier!*"

General Andrew Jackson

I must confess that I marvelled more than once at the unstudied elegance of his language and even more at the apparently spontaneous promptings of his gallantry.

Livingston was not the only man in New Orleans who was surprised at Jackson's adaptability.

Chapter XXII

THE PIRATES BECOME PATRIOTS

GENERAL JACKSON had come directly to Louisiana after his triumphs in Florida. On the Alabama River, he had gathered four thousand men together—regulars, the Mississippi dragoons, and troops from Tennessee—and in early November he had attacked two forts at Pensacola which the Spaniards had allowed the English to garrison. The British forces were driven to their ships, in which they promptly retired; and the Indian allies of the British were chased into the interior. It was just at the time of this rout that Jackson had warned Governor Claiborne of the English fleet moving toward the Louisiana coast.

As soon as he arrived in New Orleans, Jackson took count of the resources for defense. It was easy enough to do. There was Patterson's small navy, the weak Fort St.

COURTYARD OF MADAME POREÉ'S HOUSE

IN ROYAL STREET, NEW ORLEANS

The Pirates Become Patriots

Philip, on the Mississippi, and Fort Petites Coquilles on the Rigolets—as yet unfinished; Ross's seven hundred regulars, and one thousand militia mustered in only after many imperative calls. Here was a desperate situation—and twelve thousand picked troops were on their way to attack the city.

Jackson set to work on a close inspection of the men and their arms. The arms were inadequate, the supply of ammunition pitifully small. Worse, there was a shortage of flints for the guns, and the weapons were virtually useless.

Letters describing this situation were despatched at once to Washington, but there was small hope of securing the necessary supplies in time. Jackson dictated these letters to his military secretary, Edward Livingston.

Either from Livingston, or from other source, Jean Lafitte learned of the contents of those letters. And, as he sat there in the cottage of his mistress, he realized that he had one more card left to play in his game with the authorities. For, hidden safely in a secret storehouse in the marshes, not far from "The Temple," he had a supply of flints and ammunition. This storehouse was unknown and unsuspected by Patterson and Ross—and it was also unknown to Grymes and Livingston.

The next day Jean Lafitte called on General Jackson.

There is no record of that meeting, although there are scores of fictional accounts. Nor is even the place of the meeting definitely known. Some historians say that the two men met in the Cabildo; another writer asserts that they met in a room on the second floor of the Exchange Coffee House at Chartres and Saint Louis streets.

It really does not matter, for we do know that the two men met, talked, and immediately understood each other. The upshot of the conference was that Jackson accepted Lafitte's aid, and thanked him for it. He also accepted gladly the seven thousand five hundred pistol flints which Lafitte proffered, and these flints were put into the militia guns, weapons which would have been almost useless otherwise.

Only a short time before Jackson had spoken of the Baratarians as "hellish banditti," but not now. The jails were opened and the men emerged, and were armed and sent into camp. Dominique You and Beluche, pirates yesterday, were captains now. Both were skilled artillerists.

Word was sent to Last Island, and the smugglers came into the city in groups to volunteer for service. Jean and Pierre Lafitte were transformed overnight from hunted men to patriots. All proceedings against them were suspended.

Some of the Baratarians were sent to man the siege-guns of forts Petites Coquilles, St. John and St. Philip, and others were enrolled in a body of artillery under Beluche and Dominique. It is amusing to note that in one of General Jackson's subsequent reports, the Baratarians are referred to as "these privateers." They are no longer "hellish banditti."

The Pirates Become Patriots

What Claiborne, Ross and Patterson thought is not recorded. But Grymes and Livingston must have smiled to themselves. As for Jackson—he put the city under martial law and did as he pleased.

Soldiers and actors have at least one important trait in common: the ability to transform themselves in an instant from the men that they are into the men that they are expected to be—and the better the soldier or actor, the more complete is this instantaneous change.

During the New Orleans campaign Jackson had scarcely sufficient strength to stand upright without support. The disease contracted in the Alabama swamps had reduced his body to emaciation; he was almost a skeleton, unable to digest his food, unable to sleep, and tortured by constant fever. He would lie on a sofa in the room adjoining his office at headquarters, his eyes half closed, his breath coming painfully, his sallow face flushed; chills shook his body, and he suffered that unremitting pain which only the sufferer from malaria knows—a pain of both mind and body, day after day, night after dismal night.

Yet, in a moment, Jackson would spring up, call for his horse and ride out to inspect the troops. Again, he would sit, hour after hour, with his aides, mapping out a campaign, working so tirelessly that the officers were exhausted.

At half past one o'clock in the afternoon of December

23rd, the sentry announced the arrival of three gentlemen who had come galloping down the street in hot haste, and who desired immediate audience with the general. These visitors were Major Gabrielle Villeré, son of Major-General Villeré, Colonel De la Ronde, and Dussan La Croix, and they brought the news of the approach of the vanguard of the British army, which was at that hour encamped on the Villeré plantation, nine miles down the Mississippi.

When the men had finished their exciting story, General Jackson rose. His body was so wasted by disease that he swayed and placed his hand upon the table for support. But as the men watched they saw his body stiffen; the lines smoothed themselves out of his face, and he seemed in a moment to become well. More than that. He seemed suddenly in fine spirits. He called for wine, and took a glass himself as the three visitors drank. Then he summoned his secretary and aides, and turning to them he said:

"Gentlemen, the British are below. We must fight them to-night."

He then dispatched a messenger to each of the corps under his command, ordering them to break camp quickly and march to the positions assigned to them: General Carroll to the head of Bayou Bienvenu, Governor Claiborne to a point further up the Gentilly Road—a road which leads from the Chef Menteur to New Orleans. The

The Pirates Become Patriots

rest of the troops he ordered to a plantation just below the city. Commodore Patterson was also sent for and requested to prepare the *Carolina* for weighing anchor and dropping down the river.

Having issued his orders, he sat down to his dinner. He took a little rice; it was all that he could eat, so ill he was. Then he lay down upon a sofa and closed his eyes. In half an hour he was in the saddle. He did not sleep again for more than seventy hours.

Before three o'clock he had stationed himself on horseback before Fort St. Charles—at the place where the old United States Mint building stands to-day—where he waited to see the troops pass on their way to the vicinity of the enemy's position, and to give his final orders to the various commanders.

And what a strange and polyglot army it was. There passed in review not only the Creole and English-speaking citizens of New Orleans, but a host of others. Lean Kentuckians came—men who had come down the Mississippi aboard flatboats, each carrying his rifle in the crook of his arm—men who had come to help protect Creole New Orleans because Louisiana was now a part of the United States. From the prairies and bayous of inland Louisiana came the bronzed Acadians, ready to take their places in the line. From the German Coast of the Mississippi came those sturdy descendants of the flaxen-haired pioneers who had come to New Orleans nearly a century before. Companies of mulattoes and negroes— "free men of color"—came bearing arms, quietly, modestly, but ready to play their part in the defense of a city which they loved equally as well as the Creoles themselves.

Surely this was a strange group of marching men that went that afternoon down the road toward Chalmette.

Jackson, swaying with fever, racked by chills, sat on his horse and watched them go.

Slowly they went by: two regiments of regulars, a few marines and artillerymen; the New Orleans riflemen; the cavalry passing in a cloud of dust; the Mississippi dragoons; the Tennesseeans in their homespun coats; the Creole troops—breathless, having run all the way from Fort St. John; the companies of colored freemen; the Baratarians; and a small group of Choctaw Indians.

That was all. Jackson had seen his entire force pass by. There were but two thousand, one hundred and thirty-one men. More than half of them had never been in action.

Twelve thousand British soldiers waited below the city.

The orders to the troops had been simple enough: To advance as far as the Rodriguez Canal, six miles from the city and two miles from the Villeré plantation; there to halt, take positions, and wait for orders to close with the enemy. The Rodriguez canal was little more than a

The Pirates Become Patriots

wide, shallow ditch, extending across the firm ground from the river to the swamp.

At the time of the departure of the troops, the city seemed cheerful. Women crowded the windows and balconies, waving their scarves and handkerchiefs; children cried out farewells. . . . But the women knew what they must expect if the American army was defeated. Hundreds of them carried daggers in their belts.

The result of the fighting on December 23rd was the saving of Louisiana; for it is almost certain, had not Jackson's forces attacked at once and with such impetuosity before the English had effected their disembarkation, that the British troops would have marched next morning against the unfortified city.

The decisive battle, however, did not come until January 8th, 1815.

It is not my intention to describe the Battle of New Orleans. There are several excellent accounts by historians, and any effort of mine could add little to what has been written already. But I do wish to tell something of Jean Lafitte and his Baratarians on that memorable eighth of January.

Jackson's lines on that day were within five miles of the city's limits, and ran from the bank of the Mississippi to the swamp. Rude defenses had been thrown up along an old mill-race or *coulée*. This parapet was mainly constructed of earthwork revetted with boards; in some places it was twenty feet thick and five feet high, and it extended for nearly a mile. Cotton bales were used at intervals, but they soon proved unsuitable as they were easily set aflame; and although many bales of cotton were destroyed in the effort to build the parapet, little good came of them.

By January 8th, Jackson had secured additional forces, and he now commanded three thousand two hundred men. The British Army of Invasion aggregated fourteen thousand four hundred and fifty men, and it is said that fully twelve thousand of these advanced to the siege of New Orleans. The British, then, outnumbered the Americans four to one, and the Englishmen were all seasoned soldiers.

The attack began at dawn, the British advancing on the left of the American line, marching forward in massed formation through an open field. Behind the parapet the Americans waited, then fired at Jackson's command, and mowed down the enemy with frightful slaughter. Historians estimate the British losses at three thousand men, killed, wounded and missing. The American losses, incredibly enough, were only thirteen killed, thirty-nine wounded and nineteen missing.

At dawn, just before the attack, as General Jackson was riding along the line, he found the battery composed of Baratarians totally undisturbed by the coming fight; the men were, in fact, making coffee in an iron pot over a small fire.

Jackson rode up to them, sniffing the delightful aroma.

THE URSULINE CONVENT BECAME A HOSPITAL

A RUINED PLANTATION NEAR THE BATTLE-FIELD

The Pirates Become Patriots

"That smells good," he said. "It is better coffee than we get. Where did it come from? Did you *smuggle* it in?"

Dominique You shrugged his expressive shoulders, grinning.

"That may be . . . ." he said, then turning to the man who was dripping the coffee he said: "Fill a cup for the Zhenerale."

Jackson, sitting on his horse, sipped the hot, black liquid and found it delicious. He turned to his aide and said:

"I wish I had fifty such guns on this line, with five hundred such devils as those fellows behind them."

He was thinking of the battle which had taken place on January 1st, when Dominique You and Beluche distinguished themselves by handling cannon that out-shot the trained artillerists of the British forces. And, later, Jackson said, as he watched Dominique and his men: "If I were ordered to storm the gates of hell, with Captain Dominique as my lieutenant, I would have no misgivings of the result!"

Shortly after the firing began Jackson rode for a second time near the battery command by Dominique. Suddenly he reined in his horse and shouted:

"What! What! By God! What is the matter? Why have you ceased firing?"

"But of course, Zhenerale . . ." Dominique shrugged

his shoulders. "The powder is good for nothing; it is fit only to shoot blackbirds with, not redcoats."

Jackson turned in his saddle and spoke to one of his aides: "Tell the ordnance officer that I will have him shot in five minutes as a traitor if Dominique complains any more of his powder." And he galloped away.

When he returned, Dominique's battery was blazing away furiously. "Ha! Friend Dominique," cried the General, "I see you're hard at work."

"Pretty good work, too," Dominique replied, laughing. "And I think that the redcoats have discovered by this time that there has been a change in gunpowder."

There are half-a-dozen similar stories.

Pierre Lafitte was given a position of trust on that morning . . . and Jean Lafitte had been sent with a vessel to guard against a rear attack from the Mexican Gulf. With a company made up of members of his Baratarians, he was stationed near "The Temple."

Because Jean Lafitte was not in the line of American forces early in the morning of January 8th, certain writers have declared that he evaded service in the defense of New Orleans. This is not only untrue, but foolish, for Jackson's own report of the battle gives Jean all credit for bravery and valor. In addition, there is a letter which proves that Jackson thought of Jean Lafitte as one of his ablest men on that morning, a century ago.

On the bank of the Mississippi opposite to the point

The Pirates Become Patriots

where the battle was being fought, the British had attacked a small detachment of American troops and had succeeded in routing them. Jackson was as yet unaware of the tremendous slaughter that his troops had caused in the British ranks, and feared that they would renew their attack later in the day. Consequently he wished to strengthen his forces on the opposite bank of the river. He sent Jean Lafitte and General Humbert (the same General Humbert who had behaved so badly at his birthday party some time before!) to aid Brigadier-General Morgan who was in command there. Two papers remain to prove the trust which Jackson placed in these two men. The first is the pass which was given Lafitte and Humbert to allow them to cross the river. The second is this letter:

Headquarters, 7th Military District, Jan. 8, 1815

Sir:

This will be handed you by Mr. Lafitte whom I have sent to you as a man acquainted with the geography of the country on your side of the river, and will be able to afford you any information you may want with respect to the canals and passes by which the enemy may attempt to penetrate. I have also sent General Humbert, a man in whose bravery I have unbounded confidence, for the purpose of carrying the enemy at the point of the bayous. It is my determination they shall be dislodged at all events and I rely upon your determination with the aid I have sent you to accomplish it. They are not more than 400 strong and your task not a difficult one; we

Lafitte the Pirate

have held them here at all points with a loss on their side
of at least a thousand men.

ANDREW JACKSON,
Major General Commanding

To Brigadier General Morgan,
Right Bank of Mississippi.

It appears that Jean Lafitte must have speedily returned from "The Temple" after establishing the fact
that the British were not to attack from that quarter, for
there are the statements of half a dozen men which tell
of seeing him within the American lines at Chalmette at
eleven o'clock in the morning. He crossed the river with
General Humbert before noon, hastening to aid General
Morgan.

Nearly every man whose name has been mentioned in
this chronicle was in the American line with Jackson at
the Battle of New Orleans. It is the one time when we
see them all together. And what a strange group they
are! Jean and Pierre Lafitte, Governor Claiborne, John
Grymes and Edward Livingston; Ross and Patterson;
Davezac and General Humbert, with his nose like a ripe
strawberry . . . Dominique You and Beluche . . . even
the "bad ones" Gambi and Chighizola, called Nez Coupé.

And whatever else one may say against the Baratarians and their companions, no one can bring the charge
of cowardice against them. In commending some of the
pirate crew, General Jackson wrote:

The Pirates Become Patriots

Captain Dominique and Beluche, lately commanding privateers of Barataria, with part of their former crews, were stationed at Batteries Three and Four. The general cannot avoid giving his warm approbation of the manner in which these gentlemen have uniformly conducted themselves while under his command and the gallantry with which they redeemed the pledge they gave at the opening of the campaign to defend the country.

The brothers Lafitte have exhibited the same courage and fidelity and the general promises that the government shall be duly appraised of their conduct.

Note well. Jackson calls the hellish banditti "these gentlemen," now.

Chapter *XXIII*

A LION AMONG THE LADIES

WHILE the men were fighting on the plains of Chalmette, the women of New Orleans were overcome with fear. A story had been repeated everywhere—as similar stories are always repeated in a besieged city—that, should the enemy win, no woman would be safe. The toast of the British army, it was said, was the open threat: "Beauty and Booty!" And the Creoles were sure that, if the American forces were defeated, the women would fall immediate victims of violence, rape and murder.

Perhaps it was true; perhaps it was not—but every woman in New Orleans believed it.

A hundred or more ladies—"the flowers of society" —gathered at the residence of Madame Poreé—a house which is still standing at the corner of Royal and Du-

A Lion Among the Ladies

maine streets and spent the night prior to January 8th.
Some of them wrote about it afterwards, and from all
accounts the night was terrible indeed. They huddled together in the large parlors, behind the tight-barred windows. Candles were burning, and the women knelt, pray-
ing the long hours through. They waited, their rosaries in
their hands, for morning.

Shortly after dawn came the sound of cannonading,
and many became hysterical, shrieking, fainting. Let me
quote a little:

We prayed aloud in unison . . . we promised eternal
prayers, if our lives and the city were saved . . . our moans,
our shrieks and our prayers to the Blessed Virgin filled the
air. . . . Some fainted and lay as they fell, as the others
were too preoccupied to attend them. . . . At last the firing
ceased. What now? We looked at each other in terror, then
returned to our prayers with renewed fervor. . . .

At last there was a sound of a horseman galloping
down the deserted street. Madame Poreé opened a window and peered out. There was a cry. She flung the
window wide and the ladies rushed out upon the balcony.

Bang! Bang! All along the street, shutters were flying open. Every balcony was filled with women, leaning
forward, waiting. . . . A young Creole on a foam-
flecked horse dashed toward them. Before Madame
Poreé's house he drew rein. The horse reared, and the
young man shouted: "Victory! Victory!"

Lafitte the Pirate

In the Ursuline convent, the nuns listened to the cannonading, and with anxious eyes they watched from their dormer-windows as the smoke rose from the battle-field. All night long they had knelt at their chapel altar before their precious image "Our Lady of Prompt Succor." At dawn they carried the statue outside and placed it over the door, to keep out the enemy. Twice before she had saved them—twice, when nearly the whole of the city had burned—and on this day she saved them again, or so the Ursulines will tell you to-day.

When the news of the victory came, they cried out with glad thanksgiving—and went immediately to work. They threw open the convent, turning the school-rooms into infirmaries for sick and wounded of both armies.

Nor were the Creole and American ladies of New Orleans less quick to offer aid. As soon as their safety was assured, they ordered out their carriages, and many drove at once to the battle-field, laden with bandages, bedding, pillows for the wounded. Chief among them were Mesdames Claiborne and Livingston. . . . And by the services of these women many lives were saved. When the bandages were exhausted, they tore up their petticoats. They worked tirelessly until far into the night . . . and for many days afterwards. When the hospitals were filled, they took the wounded into their homes.

On the 23rd of January New Orleans celebrated in public thanksgiving. The Place D'Armes was decorated;

A Lion Among the Ladies

an arch of triumph was supported by six Corinthian columns festooned with evergreens and flowers. Young girls representing Liberty and Justice stood beside it, and beside them, posed upon pedestals, two cherubs upheld a laurel wreath. From the arch to the door of the Church of Saint Louis stood two lines of young ladies, representing the various States and Territories . . . "the loveliest young ladies of the city, dressed in white, with blue veils fastened with silver stars on their brows, each one holding a banner emblazoned with her national title, in the other a basket tied with blue ribbon and filled with flowers. Behind each, a lance stuck in the ground bore a shield with the motto and seal of the state or territory represented, and the lances were festooned together with garlands of flowers and evergreens."

At the church door the Catholic clergy waited in festive robes.

It must have been very grand indeed. One wonders what Jackson thought of it all.

The square was crowded, and at the stroke of the hour appointed, the general entered the river gate, followed by his staff. There were salvos of artillery, bursts of music, shouting and cheering.

But there were men (then, as now) who regarded the whole festival with a critical eye and were not unamused by some of the grandeur. Vincent Nolte, in his "Fifty Years in Both Hemispheres," dismisses the ceremony like this:

Lafitte the Pirate

Jackson brought back our little army to the city. A Te Deum was sung in the cathedral, at the doors of which the most prominent of the Catholic clergy received the general, and Madame Livingston, with studied enthusiasm, did herself the pleasure of setting a laurel crown upon his head, which, however, the destroyer of Indians, unused to similar marks of honor, somewhat unwillingly put away.

Other writers say the cherubs crowned him; still others say that Abbé Dubourg put the crown on Jackson's head. Nolte, of course, was a prejudiced observer, as he hated both Jackson and Livingston, although he had himself served as a volunteer in the defense of New Orleans. Nevertheless, it is just as well to inject a little matter-of-fact comment into the magnificent descriptions of all the others.

There was a ball that night.

The French Exchange had been elaborately decorated for the occasion; the upper part was arranged for dancing, and the lower floor for supper. There were flowers, colored lamps and "transparencies with inscriptions." One of these transparencies read: "Jackson and Victory: they are but one!"

And the general commented somewhat grimly: "Why not 'Hickory and Victory?' "

Vincent Nolte, who was a member of the committee in charge of the ball, cannot restrain his ill-temper when he describes certain things which took place that night. For example:

A Lion Among the Ladies

After supper we were treated to a most delicious *pas de deux* by the conqueror and his spouse. The lady explains by her enormous corpulence the French saying: "She knows how far the skin can be stretched." To see these two figures, the general a long, haggard man, with limbs like a skeleton, and Madame la Generale, a short fat dumpling, bobbing opposite each other to the wild melody of "Possum up de Gum Tree," and endeavoring to make a spring into the air, was very remarkable, and far more edifying a spectacle than any European ballet could have been.

But, all deprecating remarks aside, the ball was memorable in New Orleans social life. It was perhaps the only occasion when the rigid society met and enjoyed those not socially blessed, but for the moment important because of the part they had played in the American victory at Chalmette. And it was perhaps the only time that the Creole ladies of New Orleans—and the American ladies as well—saw Jean and Pierre Lafitte. And Jean talked with them.

There are ten or more references to Jean Lafitte in the letters which have fallen into my hands in compiling the material for this book. Each lady who spoke to "that handsome man" has some delightful detail to give us.

"I had heard," writes one, "that M. Lafitte had no use for women, which seemed somewhat odd; but I am sure that those who told me were incorrectly informed. He is a tall man of extraordinary good looks, dark and slender. His hands and feet are small, and he has a look in those

Lafitte the Pirate

dark eyes that few women could resist. . . . I talked with him for a moment, and he told me that there was no truth *at all* in the stories which have been told against him. He was never a pirate, and his only crime was privateering, which he explains by saying that he has deep hatred for Spain, owing to cruelty which he suffered from the Spanish when confined in a fortress at Havana. . . ."

Another lady has this to say:

"I have met the famous privateer, Jean Lafitte, and found him a handsome man of about thirty-five years; he confided in me that he was a widower and has cared little for women since the death of his beautiful young wife. He seemed very sad as he said this."

Still another: "Mr. Lafitte told my husband that he has long hated the British, owing to their cruel treatment of himself when a young man. I did not have opportunity to talk with him myself. He is a fine-looking gentleman, and one calculated to make a woman's heart beat. . . . He is a bachelor."

Odd, but none of the ladies mention the cross-eyed Pierre. And still more peculiar that they tell such widely varying stories of what Jean Lafitte has told them. We can draw but two conclusions: one, that all the ladies were so upset by meeting the hero that they reported incorrectly the things he said; the other conclusion—and one which seems more logical—is that Lafitte told each woman a different tale, working on the principle that it pays to tell women what they want to hear. To one he was

A Lion Among the Ladies

a bachelor; to another a widower; to a third he said that he could not love again after an unfortunate affair in his youth. He hated Spain, or he hated England—either hatred was good enough to explain that he was not a pirate, but a privateer. He was all things to all women that night—and they never saw him again.

He was at the peak of his fame that evening. Wherever he went he was pointed out, discussed, admired. He was seen talking with his former enemy, Governor Claiborne, and those who listened to the conversation said that the two men were joking about the rewards that they had offered for each other's capture.

So animated the men became that others soon joined them, and a gay group stood laughing there, each uplifted hand holding a glass. Brigadier-General Coffee came up. He was Jackson's brother-in-law, and had distinguished himself at the battle. Claiborne introduced him to Lafitte.

Coffee hesitated, trying to place the name, or perhaps he was trying to reconcile the name with the very elegant gentleman who stood before him. At any rate, he hesitated. Lafitte, furious at the fancied insult, stepped forward and said: "Lafitte, the pirate!"

Coffee apologized, explained and shook hands. And all was serene. But those who heard this bit of by-play had good reason to remember it later on.

Chapter XXIV

REINSTATED TO CITIZENSHIP

LAFITTE's lawyers wasted no time. Letters from Edward Livingston and John Grymes were sent at once to President Madison, asking for the promised pardon for the Baratarians, and the President issued a proclamation reinstating them to citizenship only eighteen days after Jackson's army returned in triumph to New Orleans.

Like nearly every other paper relating to the Baratarians it is interesting in detail, so it is given here in its entirety:

A PROCLAMATION.—Among the many evils produced by the wars, which, with little intermission, have afflicted Europe, and extended their ravages into other quarters of the globe, for a period exceeding twenty years, the dispersion of

Reinstated to Citizenship

a considerable portion of the inhabitants of different countries, in sorrow and in want, has not been the least injurious to human happiness, nor the least severe in the trial of human virtue.

I had been long ascertained, that many foreigners flying from the dangers of their home, and that some citizens, forgetful of their duty, had co-operated in forming an establishment on the island of Barataria near the mouth of the river Mississippi, for the purpose of a clandestine and lawless trade. The government of the United States caused the establishment to be broken up and destroyed; and, having obtained the means of designating the offenders of every description, it only remained to answer the demands of justice, by inflicting an exemplary punishment.

But it has since been represented, that the offenders have manifested a sincere penitence; that they have abandoned the prosecution of the worst cause for the support of the best; and particularly, that they have exhibited, in the defence of New Orleans, unequivocal traits of courage and fidelity. Offenders, who have refused to become the associates of the enemy in the way, upon the most seducing terms of invitation; and who have aided to repel his hostile invasion of the territory of the United States; can no longer be considered as objects of punishment, but as objects of a generous forgiveness.

It has, therefore, been seen with great satisfaction, that the general assembly of the state of Louisiana earnestly recommend those offenders to the benefit of a full pardon; And in compliance with that recommendation, as well as in consideration of all the other extraordinary circumstances of the case, I, James Madison, president of the United States of America, do issue this proclamation, hereby granting, publishing and declaring, a free and full pardon of all offences committed in

Lafitte the Pirate

violation of any act or acts of the congress of the said United States, touching the revenue, trade and navigation thereof, or touching the intercourse and commerce of the United States with foreign nations, at any time before the eighth day of January, in the present year one thousand eight hundred and fifteen, by any person or persons whatsoever, being inhabitants of New Orleans and the adjacent country, or being inhabitants of the said island of Barataria and the places adjacent: Provided, That every person claiming the benefit of this full pardon, in order to entitle himself thereto, shall produce a certificate in writing from the governor of the state of Louisiana, stating that such person has aided in the defence of New Orleans and the adjacent country, during the invasion thereof as aforesaid.

And I do hereby further authorise and direct all suits, indictments, and prosecutions, for fines, penalties, and for forfeitures, against any person, or persons, who shall be entitled to the benefit of this full pardon forthwith to be stayed, discontinued and released: And all civil officers are hereby required, according to the duties of their respective stations, to carry this proclamation into immediate and faithful execution.

DONE at the city of Washington, the sixth day of February, in the year one thousand eight hundred and fifteen, and of the independence of the United States the thirty-ninth.

JAMES MADISON

By the President,

JAS. MONROE, Acting secretary of state.

It is at this point that the novelists, and other writers of fiction concerning Jean Lafitte, pause, smile, and grasp their pens with renewed vigor. This is the climax. There

A BARATARIAN VILLAGE

A LANE AT GRANDE ISLE

Reinstated to Citizenship

is little left to write now, aside from that happy phrase: "And he lived happily ever after."

It is at this point that novelists let their brave pirate-patriot find that "the love of a good woman is the greatest thing in the world." And so on, and so on. Jean Lafitte is happy now. And why not? Isn't he a hero? Isn't he an American? Isn't that enough?

Unfortunately, these conjectures are the exact opposite of truth. Jean Lafitte was far from happy. Citizenship, aside from a pardon for past misdemeanors, meant little to him. His whole life had been turned topsy-turvy; Barataria had been destroyed; his men were scattered; his fortune had been seized by Ross and Patterson. He had not the slightest desire to marry a noble woman and settle down. He appears to have been fairly well satisfied with his quadroon mistress Catherine Villars, certainly he was fond of her, but she was not a driving force in his life. Rather, she kept him satisfied, and she gave no trouble . . . his real interests lay elsewhere. It was power that he wanted, and it was power that he was determined to have. Barataria was destroyed, very well. He would build another Barataria. There is nothing to indicate that, for one instant, he considered changing his mode of life. He and his men had done their best to defend New Orleans against the British. Now he wanted his property returned to him.

Livingston and Grymes brought suit to recover the vessels and merchandise seized by the United States at

Lafitte the Pirate

Grande Terre. In order to do this, they must prove Jean Lafitte's patriotism. Accordingly they filed with the District Court of Louisiana the entire correspondence which had passed between the British officers and Lafitte, and also the correspondence with John Blanque. (For years these papers remained a part of the court record; then, like so many other papers pertaining to the Baratarians, they disappeared. Some years ago these letters turned up in a curio shop in New Orleans. They were purchased by a private collector and subsequently sold again to E. A. Parsons. They now form a part of his remarkable private library.)

But those men who now had possession of the spoils from Barataria were not to be caught napping. Before Lafitte's suit to recover his property could come up for trial, they sold the vessels and merchandise at public auction. Now, let Grymes and Livingston sue the United States for recompense. That was not so easy to do.

Jean Lafitte still had money, and he had wealthy friends. At the auction of the vessels, Sauvinet bought them in! Had Lafitte intended to settle down and marry a noble woman and become a good citizen of the United States, he would have had little use for such a fleet.

But he had other plans.

Chapter XXV

PUBLIC OPINION VEERS ABOUT

WE have spoken before of the mercurial temperament of the people of New Orleans. A particularly striking example of this quality was exhibited shortly after Jackson's victory at Chalmette.

The English had withdrawn their forces from the Louisiana coast, and immediately the people were happy that the danger had passed. The British had been defeated; the Americans were victorious; that's all there was to it. Jackson, however, thought it best to be on guard, for the enemy had struck another blow, and Fort Bowyer, at Mobile, had surrendered to the English forces on February 12th.

News of the treaty of peace between Great Britain and the United States came to New Orleans, and the fol-

Lafitte the Pirate

lowing handbills were distributed by the editor of the Louisiana Gazette:

A truce-boat from Admiral Cochrane, commander of the English fleet, has just brought to General Jackson official news of a treaty concluded at Ghent, between the United States and Great Britain, and the request for a cessation of hostilities.

The city was still under martial law and Jackson was supreme in power. When he saw the handbills, he was furious, and wrote at once to Mr. Cotten, the editor of the paper, demanding that a second notice be distributed immediately denying this. Jackson explained that he believed the news to be a trick by the English, and that he would accept no notice of peace as official until it came to him from the President of the United States.

The people of New Orleans, however, believed the news—which proved subsequently to be perfectly true—and there was great dissatisfaction expressed. Every one was tired of martial law. The volunteers had seen all the service they wanted, and wished to return to their homes. There was open discontent and countless applications for discharge. To all this, Jackson turned a deaf ear.

But in the army there were many French citizens, and when they could not obtain discharge in the regular way, they made application to the French consul at New Orleans. These were taken to Jackson who countersigned them and permitted the bearers to be discharged. But

Public Opinion Veers About

within a few days there were so many such orders that Jackson suspected them to be improperly granted. This made him still more angry, and on February 28th he issued a general order commanding all French subjects to leave the city and not be nearer than the town of Baton Rouge. This included the consul.

There was consternation in French-speaking New Orleans. Matters reached a climax when a newspaper published a communication calling on those expelled by Jackson to cease being guided by military tribunals and seek redress and appeal in the regular courts of Louisiana. Jackson's fury was intense; he secured the name of the anonymous writer from the editor of the paper, and ordered his arrest. A well-known Creole gentleman, M. Louaillier, was the author; he was also a member of the Legislature, and had taken active part in defending New Orleans against invasion.

Louaillier was arrested in Maspero's Exchange Coffee House on March 5th, and confined in the barracks. United States District Judge Dominic A. Hall granted a writ of *habeas corpus*. This produced an explosion. Jackson ordered Judge Hall arrested and locked up. Some days later a court-martial tried Louaillier, on charges of "mutiny, exciting mutiny, general misconduct, being a spy, illegal misconduct, disobedience to orders, unsoldierlike behavior and violating martial law." All charges were based upon his article in the paper. The court-martial freed him, but Jackson, still enraged, re-

Lafitte the Pirate

fused to release him from prison. Foreseeing the result of Judge Hall's trial, Jackson had him removed from the city.

Two days after the Judge was banished, New Orleans was awakened by cannon shots. A courier had arrived bringing the official news of the peace treaty from the President of the United States, and carrying an order to Jackson to pardon all military offenders. Louaillier and Judge Hall were released, and the French Consul returned to his post. On the 14th, General Jackson began necessary measures to disband the troops; in his farewell address he stated that his harsh behavior was a part of the necessary course of war. But the Creoles were still incensed. Public opinion, that fickle jade, had turned away from him. And, as astonishing as it appears now, Jackson was tried for contempt of court, found guilty and fined one thousand dollars.

Gayarré tells us that "excitement was intense" in the city. Many expected bloodshed. A crowd gathered before the place of trial. Some were merely curious, others were friends and admirers of Jackson. When he emerged from the court-room, after having paid his fine, he was met with cheers.

The crowd was composed largely of the Baratarians, with Dominique You and Beluche in command. Jackson was lifted upon the shoulders of the men and carried to Maspero's Exchange where the cheering crowd demanded a speech. He spoke briefly and without rancor.

Public Opinion Veers About

A purse was made up, and the thousand dollar fine was returned to him; but he declined it, and asked that the money be distributed to the widows and children of those men who had lost their lives in the Battle of New Orleans. (It was nearly thirty years later, in 1843, that the Congress of the United States refunded to Jackson the amount of his fine, together with interest, amounting to $2,700.)

It is evident that Jackson's denunciation of the Legislature (when that body was accused of being willing to surrender to the enemy) had made many enemies for him. When the Legislature convened, a most remarkable set of resolutions were passed: these resolutions praised every one who had any part in defending the city, *except* Andrew Jackson. Another resolution to present him with a sabre valued at $800, as a testimonial of gratitude for his defense of New Orleans, was passed by the lower house, but was rejected by the Senate.

Nor was Jackson the only one to suffer from the mercurial public opinion of New Orleans. A change had come over the city with regard to Jean Lafitte. He sensed it immediately, and was somewhat puzzled. Even at the time when he had been outlawed by the authorities, he had been a popular figure. He had always possessed a romantic quality which pleased the Creoles. But now there were whispers about him. More than that.

There was one story that had been forgotten in the

excitement of the siege, but it was revived now. This was the story of the jewels and linens of the Creole lady which had been found in the merchandise taken from the storehouse at Grande Terre. Many believed that the poor woman had been captured by pirates and had been murdered; how else did Jean Lafitte come into possession of her personal belongings? In vain did his friends try to explain. Perhaps, they said, the lady was captured by pirates and murdered; but was Jean Lafitte to blame? The articles might have come innocently to his storehouse. . . . Perhaps his men had captured a pirate vessel and had taken these articles among the loot. Perhaps . . . there were many explanations. But they were met with shrugs of disbelief.

His suit to recover damages from the Federal Government was another thing which laid Lafitte open to criticism. Creole New Orleans was becoming Americanized, and the American point of view was unfavorable to such procedure by the Baratarian. His motives and even his patriotism were questioned now. Why, asked his detractors, did he continue to visit Grande Terre? Why was he again in possession of his fleet? Was he attempting to reëstablish his pirate kingdom? If so, they would have none of it.

And before this intangible enemy, Lafitte was as powerless as Jackson had been.

Chapter *XXVI*

THE SPANISH SPIES

IRONICALLY enough, the Battle of New Orleans had been useless, for a treaty of peace between England and the United States was signed prior to the fighting in Louisiana. But after the victory of the American forces at Chalmette, the spirit of revolution remained in the air. The fires of the Napoleonic wars in Europe had kindled blazes in the Western hemisphere; and in Louisiana there were many men still eager to fight. The British having gone home again, these warlike Louisianians turned their attention to aiding the colonies of Spain in their struggle for independence. Several small filibustering expeditions marched off to Texas and Mexico. Claiborne issued another of his proclamations, urging all citizens of the

Lafitte the Pirate

United States to remain strictly neutral—for diplomatic relations with Spain were about to be resumed, having been suspended since 1808.

Not long after the Battle of New Orleans, a Spanish consul arrived in New Orleans.

While diplomatic relations with Spain had been suspended Lafitte's destruction of Spanish vessels might have been considered privateering; but now such attacks upon Spain must be classed as piracy.

It was understood in New Orleans that the Baratarians, and Jean Lafitte in particular, were in sympathy with the Spanish revolutionists. Over and over again, Lafitte had told of his eternal hatred for Spain. Now, after doing their part in defending Louisiana, many of the former Baratarians had joined the Spanish-American patriots in Texas.

The summer and autumn of 1815 were filled with disappointment for Lafitte. His suit to recover damages from the United States hung fire: Grymes and Livingston were not hopeful, although they had filed the necessary papers in the courts, and Livingston had written to the President in the interest of his client.

Barataria was still unsafe for smuggling or privateering, as it was closely watched, and although many of Lafitte's men had returned to their homes on Grande Isle and at the old pirate village of Cheniere Caminada, they were now only fishermen. True, they were bored with this peaceful occupation, and were ready and willing to

The Spanish Spies

return to smuggling and other illicit operations, but Lafitte knew that such a course was impossible as yet. Later
perhaps, but not now. He did not, for a moment, consider giving up New Orleans as a market for ill-gotten
goods, and he intended to use the labyrinthine bayous of
Barataria as before; but he must find another spot for
headquarters—a place of safety, beyond the jurisdiction
of the United States.

He began, therefore, to cast about for new scenes for
his operations; and, having purchased through Sauvinet
the eight vessels which had been captured by Ross and
Patterson and sold as prizes, he embarked for Port au
Prince. Pierre Lafitte, Dominique You, and many of his
men went with him.

There can be no doubt that they had resolved upon a
course of piracy.

Dominique You was a Creole of Santo Domingo, and
he and the Lafittes expected to be welcomed in the West
Indian islands. But their anticipations proved futile.
Their reputation had gone before them. In addition, the
island officials were frank in saying that too many suspicious captures had been attributed to the Baratarians.
They were allowed to revictual their ships. The Haytian
ports were closed against them.

A small group of Spanish-American patriots were at
the island of Galveston on the Texas coast, and the Lafitte brothers decided to go there. But it was at this time
that they parted company with Dominique You. The rea-

Lafitte the Pirate

son for this separation is not clear; nor is the date of the parting known; but You played no part in their subsequent history.

For some reason, the Lafittes did not go at once to Galveston, although it is probable that they visited the island on a tour of inspection. The fleet returned to the waters of Barataria, and the brothers and Dominique went back to New Orleans.

The records are scanty, and there is no way of knowing just what happened then; but we do know that Jean Lafitte was an embittered man. His old prestige was gone; he had lost his leader Dominique; his men were scattered; he had no place for his headquarters; he even seems to have been pressed for money for the first time in his career.

For now we come to the strangest part of the history of the brothers.

They became spies for Spain.

We have seen that Jean was a past-master in double-dealing. His adroit betrayal of the British officers at Grande Terre was an excellent example of this; and although from the American point of view, his actions at that time were exemplary, the English version of the story paints him as the blackest of traitors. Heretofore his loyalty to his men had been admirable; it seems to me that this loyalty was his finest characteristic; but in becoming a Spanish spy, he was, in a sense, betraying them. . . .

The Spanish Spies

I will not attempt to justify, nor even explain his decision; I can only make the flat statement that he became a spy. There is abundant proof of this in the archives of Spain. It is evident, from subsequent letters he wrote to the Spanish governor of Havana, that he expected Spain to furnish him with an army to use as he saw fit at Galveston. But the governor was his match in adroitness, and although he appears to have promised much, the army was not forthcoming; Jean Lafitte was still urging him to send aid against "these American gentlemen" as late as 1819. The letters will be quoted in their proper places.

There was a strong bond of affection between Pierre and Jean. They had been partners in all their previous dealings, and they were together in this. As usual, Jean seems to be the leader, but Pierre does his share. The letters in the Spanish archives are plain enough. Sometimes in the records, the names are given the Spanish spelling, Juan and Pedro. There is, however, no question of the identity of the men.

What a game Jean Lafitte was playing now!

It seems highly improbable that he acted honestly in his dealings with Spain, although he received money from Fatio, the Spanish consul at New Orleans; and in return he betrayed the movements of the Spanish-American patriots in Texas. It was now impossible for him to act honestly with his own men, whose sympathies were with the revolutionists. His men, of course, did not know that he was a spy, and perhaps he realized that Spaniards keep their secrets well; it may be that he felt safe enough.

But puzzling questions immediately suggest themselves: How did he gain the confidence of the new Spanish consul at New Orleans, and of the Governor of Havana? His warfare against Spanish shipping was well known, and how did he explain it, satisfactorily? Did he manage to convince them that his numerous public assertions of hatred for Spain were all lies, told for his own protection?

These are questions that I cannot answer, and perhaps they will never be answered; for, owing to the need for strict secrecy in the records of spies in the Spanish archives, the information is fragmentary.

There is a story told by several writers that, shortly after the Battle of New Orleans, Jean Lafitte went to Washington, spent sixty thousand dollars in "entertaining society" and became a prominent figure at the capital. I have not been able to verify this, but from information in the Spanish archives, I do know that he was in New Orleans and the vicinity of Galveston from November 1815 to June 1816, but that Pierre Lafitte visited Washington and Philadelphia in December, 1815.

He left New Orleans at the end of November on business connected with the brothers' new occupation as spies. In order to offer a plausible reason for his journey, he carried with him a letter from his brother, written in French, and addressed to James Madison, President of the United States. It appears that, an English translation

The Spanish Spies

of the letter was necessary, and that such a translation was subsequently made; for both letters are to be found in the files at Washington known as "The Madison papers." The signature of the English letter is, obviously, not that of Jean Lafitte. Perhaps Pierre signed it, perhaps the translator. The letter follows, and we see that Jean has lost none of his ability for "making phrases."

Washington, December 27th, 1815

President:

Encouraged by the benevolent disposition of your Excellency, I beg to be permitted to state a few facts which are not generally known in this part of the Union, and in the meantime solicit the recommendation of your Excellency to the honorable Secretary of the Treasury of the United States whose decision could not be but in my favor, if he only was well acquainted with my disinterested conduct during the last attempt of the Britannic forces on Louisiana. At the epoch that State was threatened of an invasion, I disregarded any other consideration which did not tend to its safety, and therefore retained my vessels at Barataria in spite of representations of my officers who were for making sail for Carthagena, as soon as they were informed that an expedition was preparing in New Orleans to come against us.

For my part I conceived that nothing else but disconfidence in me could induce the authorities of the State to proceed with so much severity at a time that I had not only offered my services, but likewise acquainting them with the progress of the enemy and expecting instructions which were promised to me, I permitted my officers and crews to secure what was their own, assuring them that if my property should be seized I had

Lafitte the Pirate

not the least apprehension of the equity of the United States once they would be convinced of the sincerity of my conduct.

My view in preventing the departure of my vessels was in order to retain about four hundred artillery in the country which could be of the most importance for its defence. When the aforesaid expedition arrived, I abandoned all I possessed in its power, and retired with all my crews in the marshes, a few miles above New Orleans, and invited the inhabitants of the city and environs to meet at Mr. Labranche's where I acquainted them with the nature of the danger which was not far off (as may be seen by the affixed document which is attested by some of the inhabitants which were present). A few days after, a proclamation of the Government of the State permitted us to join the army which was organizing for the defence of the country.

My conduct since that period is notorious.

The country is safe and I claim no merit for having, like all the inhabitants of the State, co-operated in this welfare. In this my conduct has been dictated by the impulses of my proper sentiments. But I claim the equity of the Government of the United States upon which I always relied for the restitution of at least that portion of my property which will not deprive the treasury of the United States of any of its own funds.

For which benefit will live forever grateful, your Excellency's very respectful and very humble and obedient servant

JN. LAFITTE

His Excellency, The President of the United States

The inclosure which he mentions is not found among the Madison papers, although it may have been preserved

"THREE OAKS" PLANTATION AT CHALMETTE

SPANISH ARSENAL—ONCE THE CALABOZO

The Spanish Spies

among the papers in some other department at Washington.

Despite its fine phrases, the letter has a somewhat hollow sound; and it seems to have served no particular purpose. Grymes and Livingston had already filed suit to recover the property, and the facts of the case were known to President Madison. But the delivery of this letter, and other mysterious errands contrived to keep Pierre in Washington for some time. He also paid a visit to Philadelphia.

It may be added that the brothers never got their money back.

Meanwhile at New Orleans a less mysterious event transpired in the cottage near the ramparts. The quadroon girl Catherine Villars, when scarcely sixteen years old, gave birth to a son. The baby was baptised at the Church of Saint Louis by Father Antonio de Sedella, or "Pere Antoine" as he was affectionately called. The record states that the child is the illegitimate son of Jean Lafitte and of Catherine Villars, free woman of color. The baby was named in honor of his uncle Pierre (or Pedro, as the Spanish priest wrote it down). This mark of affection seems to have pleased the uncle; for when Marie Louise Villars presented him with a son in 1816, he returned the compliment by naming his baby Jean.

Chapter XXVII

GALVESTON

On the first of September, 1816, José Manuel de Herrera, Mexican Representative to the United States, commissioned a Frenchman, Louis d'Aury, as commander of the fleet of the Mexican Republic. A few days later Herrera and d'Aury created a government on the island of Galveston, and d'Aury received a second high-sounding title: this time he became Civil and Military Governor of the Province of Texas. The Mexican flag was raised on the island and allegiance sworn to the new government. A Court of Admiralty was set up and rude fortifications were built. By the end of October there were approximately five hundred men there, and active privateering began against Spanish commerce. The prize car-

Galveston

goes were disposed of secretly in New Orleans, brought in through the streams of Barataria. The captured vessels were renamed and became part of the Spanish-American fleet.

The Collector of Customs at New Orleans thought no more highly of d'Aury and his men than the former collector had thought of Lafitte and his followers. In a report of August 1st, 1817, he wrote:

"I deem it my duty to state that the most shameful violations of the slave acts, as well as our revenue laws, continue to be committed with impunity by a motley mixture of freebooters and smugglers at Galveston, under the Mexican flag, being in reality little less than the re-establishment of Lafitte's Baratarians, somewhat more out of the reach of justice. . . . The establishment of Commodore d'Aury was recently made with a few small schooners from Aux Cayes, manned in a great measure with refugees from Barataria, and mulattoes . . . " He then goes on to denounce the "pretended Court of Admiralty" and says that there is no evidence that the men at Galveston have any connection with the Spanish-American patriots and their activities, but that they use this as a pretext for committing piracy.

Late in 1816, that strange and unfortunate soldier of fortune, Esposa y Mina, arrived at Galveston with a force of two hundred men. His intention was to secure help from d'Aury in an expedition into Mexico via Sota la Marina. Demurring at first, d'Aury later changed his

Lafitte the Pirate

mind and joined the expedition with his men; but it was not until April 1817 that the force got underway. Mina and d'Aury quarreled and d'Aury deserted, returning with some of his followers to Matagorda. Mina continued with a force of only three hundred men. His small army was defeated by Spanish Royalists, and he was captured and executed on December 12th. With him at the time of his capture were some seventy-five Americans; only four survived.

Galveston was for a time almost deserted. This was Jean Lafitte's opportunity. He arrived there with a small fleet and a few of his former men. His vessels sailed nowadays under the Venezuelan flag. He began at once to fortify the island and effect a permanent settlement. And to his new headquarters he gave the name Campeachy.

The news of the new Lafitte establishment spread rapidly, and followers came flocking back to him. Before long his men numbered one thousand. Houses were built. There was now *Maison Rouge,* Lafitte's new dwelling, a combination of residence and fort, strongly constructed and painted bright red; cannon were visible through apertures in the upper story. Around it, a village was springing up; there were houses, a commissary, saloons, a billiard hall; there was even a boarding-house. Many of the men brought women with them—a strange and riffraff crew: there were prostitutes from New Orleans, negro women, Indian squaws, and a few decent American wives, who afterward described Campeachy as "a terrible place for a nice woman."

In July, 1817, d'Aury returned, but when he found Lafitte so strongly entrenched, he withdrew, disclaiming any responsibility for depredations which Lafitte's men might commit in the future.

The Collector of Customs at New Orleans now informs his government that Lafitte is again introducing illicit merchandise and slaves into Louisiana. He is somewhat embarrassed, and explains his embarrassment like this:

"On the part of these pirates we have to contend with, we behold an extended and organized system of enterprize, of ingenuity, of indefatigability, and of audacity, favored by a variety of local advantages, and supported by force of arms; and unless they be met by corresponding species of resistance, the results of the contest are of very simple calculation."

The government at Galveston was Communistic. Jean Lafitte, wisely enough, did not let his name appear among the officials of the Commune. But he was "bos" all the same, Ramon Espagnol, the secretary of state, treasurer and notary public, when later testifying in a New Orleans court, said: "The government . . . had neither knowledge nor belief in the existence of a Mexican Republic and the sole object of the persons comprising the establishment at Galveston was to capture Spanish property under what they called the Mexican flag,

Lafitte the Pirate

but without an idea of aiding the revolution in Mexico."

Things were prospering at Galveston when J. Randall Jones visited there in 1818 for the purpose of buying slaves. In a letter written at the time, he tells of news current in New Orleans that Lafitte had negroes to sell.

A drove had been purchased from him at *one dollar per pound* and smuggled into Louisiana. My friends wished me to let them know if any such speculations could be made, and offered to divide profits with me for my assistance.

So Mr. Jones set out for Galveston, meeting men "engaged in some revolutionary scheme" on the way. He managed to find a sloop sailing from the mouth of Trinity River to Galveston and he took passage thereon, bringing a pirogue in tow in order to ensure a safe return.

On arriving at Galveston I was introduced by the Captain of the sloop to the great Lafitte. He treated me with the most respectful attention while I staid, which was two days and two nights. There were men of all nations, and some few women. There was a large number of boats of different sizes. There was a large schooner which I was informed was a prize laden with sugar, cocoa, coffee and wines, and there was an armed schooner. Lafitte himself had a pretty good house, the balance were made hastily of planks, sails and so on. Lafitte had thrown up an earthen fort and had some cannon mounted on the bay. There was a schooner from Boston there, trading potatoes and groceries.

Galveston

I informed Lafitte of my business and he informed me that he was out of negroes, at that time, but he expected some before long.

He was a man about six feet in height, proportionately made, tolerable fair skin, his hair dark, a little gray mixed, and was a very handsome man. I was well treated by him and all his people.

Four other men have written of their visits to Campeachy in 1818; but all the accounts have the same fault; the writers insist on telling us what they think or believe, rather than what they see and hear. They all agree that Lafitte had a quadroon girl with him as housekeeper. And they explain her in various ways. Not one describes her nor tells us anything definite except that she was "handsome" or "fine-looking," or "likely." One writer says that she is Jean Lafitte's daughter; another declares that she is said to be his daughter "but such is not the case; she is the daughter of his brother and a quadroon mother." This is impossible, as the oldest of Pierre's children by Marie Villars was but six years old in 1818. Another writer assures us that the young girl is "highly educated in Canada, and is the ward of Captain Lafitte." But the fourth writer tells us something interesting; the girl's name is Jeannette.

Was this, then, Catherine Villars? She was only seventeen years old in 1818, and Jean Lafitte, already growing gray, was thirty-seven. Catherine might have been mistaken for his daughter. There is no mention of a

Lafitte the Pirate

child. I am inclined to believe that the girl at Galveston was Catherine, but there is no real proof of it.

At times, when all crews were in harbor, as many as a thousand men would gather for the island festivities; it was a motley crowd; every language was heard. There was some gaiety, much gambling, drinking, and dancing. There were also frequent fights and occasional murders. But behavior was good enough at most times, for Lafitte seemed to have a genius for handling men, and a word from him would restore order in nearly any mêlée.

The first difficulty at Galveston was with the Carancahua Indians. This small but ferocious tribe paid occasional visits to the settlement; they were ordered away for petty pilfering, and were resentful; the real trouble began when four of the men from Campeachy—a hunting party —stole a squaw and brought her back to the village with them.

The tribe attacked the settlement, and Lafitte with about two hundred men and two pieces of artillery, went out to meet them. The fighting was protracted and severe; thirty Indians were killed and many were wounded; some of Lafitte's men were killed and wounded as well. At last the Indians retreated in their canoes. A party pursued and killed more of them. After the battle there was a celebration at Campeachy, of which is said: "Lafitte relaxed somewhat his stern manners and joined the songs of the men, and was right merry." This fight with the Caranca-

Galveston

huas was known afterwards as "The Battle of the Three Trees."

Campeachy reached the zenith of its prosperity in the summer of 1818. More buccaneers arrived, bringing their women with them; an ever-increasing number of traders came to the settlement; and there was a constant infusion of men of all nations—gamblers, thieves, murderers and other criminals who joined Lafitte's colony in order to escape punishment for crimes committed within the borders of the United States.

Numerous rich prizes were brought in, including several captured slavers loaded with Africans. Negroes were selling at a dollar a pound, an average of only one hundred and forty dollars for a man. "Doubloons," says one writer, "were as plentiful as biscuits."

But in the late summer of 1818 a tropical hurricane swept over the island, leaving death and destruction in its wake. Fourteen vessels were wrecked in the harbor and the houses of the settlement were washed away. As the storm approached and the waves rose higher and higher on the low-lying island, Jean Lafitte and some of his officers went aboard the *Tonnere* which lay at anchor in the bay, leaving *Maison Rouge,* that combination of fort and residence, for the women. Because the fort was strongly constructed, and because Lafitte's rooms on the lower floor were weather-tight and comfortable, it was thought to be the safest place. But at midnight, when the

Lafitte the Pirate

sea covered the island, and when the wind was blowing a gale, the fort collapsed. The heavy cannon in the upper story crashed down upon the women in the rooms below, and the falling timbers killed and maimed many of them. Jeannette was among the injured.

Hundreds of men lost their lives, and the next morning the beach was strewn with corpses. The financial loss was estimated at more than a million dollars. Campeachy was a water-soaked ruin.

All accounts of survivors agree that Lafitte was magnificent in those terrible days which followed the hurricane. He was tireless, and he was everywhere—assisting the injured, salvaging what was of value from the wreckage; planning for the future. His own fortune had been swept away, but he did not seem to think of that. Nor did he appear discouraged. His whole energy was devoted to caring for his men, to feeding the hungry, and to providing shelter for those who were injured or ill.

In a few days after the hurricane, the dead had been buried in the sand-hills; the wounded were housed in huts made from the wreckage of vessels, and in the remains of the fort. The damaged merchandise was sorted out from that which was worthless. So much food had been destroyed by the storm that famine threatened. How was he to feed eight hundred people? It was then that he made one of his quick and cold decisions: the negroes must be sacrificed. Many of his men had taken negro women for mistresses, and there were many slave-workmen in the camp. Now they were proving a real problem, for there was not food enough to go around.

Three days after the storm a schooner from New Orleans put in at Galveston. Lafitte took possession of her, and herded all of the negroes on board. Black women were dragged, screaming, from their white lovers and put into the hold of the vessel; others went in silence, knowing that any struggle was useless. The schooner sailed for Barataria, and approached New Orleans through the bayous. At night the negroes were smuggled into the city. The next day they were sold as slaves. In a week they were scattered and forgotten.

The departure of the negroes reduced the number of persons requiring food at Galveston; and the money from this strange sale kept the settlement from starvation.

Lafitte himself hastened to New Orleans in order to secure a new loan from his bankers. He must have been successful in this, for he returned with the supplies needed to rebuild Campeachy, and with food for the commissary.

Three vessels of his fleet were away from the island and escaped the storm. These were the *Jupiter*, the *Success* and the *Ciel Bleu*. They returned subsequently with slaves and prize-goods.

But the commune never recovered its former wealth, and after that time the men received prize money only at long intervals.

Chapter XXVIII

ALL THINGS TO ALL MEN

SHORTLY after the storm of 1818, John McHenry, an American soldier of fortune, joined the establishment at Galveston. McHenry published a memoir in DeBow's Review in October, 1853, in which he tells of this experience. He sailed with a fleet under the command of Jean Lafitte; and as this is one of the few recorded instances of the chieftain's commanding such an expedition at sea, it may be interesting to follow the voyage through.

There were three vessels in the fleet; the brig *Victoria*, a frigate which McHenry does not name, and the schooner *Blanque*. The vessels kept together, sailing down the Mexican coast, and making several unimportant captures. At Sisal, on the coast of Yucatan, they captured a large, fine schooner in the night, under the very walls of

ISLAND COTTAGES, HIDDEN AMONG THE TREES

COURTYARD OF THE NAPOLEON HOUSE,
NEW ORLEANS

the fort. This vessel proved to be a slaver, loaded with negroes. From Sisal the fleet sailed to Cape Antonio, Cuba, and on the way espied a fleet of ten merchant ships under the convoy of a Spanish frigate. Lafitte made the signal for his vessels to come alongside for consultation and asked the men if they were willing to fight or not. The men authorized one of their number—Theodore Rawlins, a Baltimorean—to announce their anxiety to give battle, as they had been out for a long time and had realized little. Lafitte then informed them that his commission from Venezuela had expired, and, if they should be taken, their fate would be that of pirates. This announcement caused much dissatisfaction, and a number of the better-class men demanded that they be given a vessel to take them to New Orleans. With great reluctance he gave them the brig *Victoria,* first taking off the armament and stripping her. After proceeding together to the island of Mugeres, the fleet separated, and the *Victoria* and her crew finally succeeded in reaching New Orleans, where they told their story and surrendered to the Customs Officials.

So ends McHenry's story.

When Lafitte reached Galveston again, he found trouble waiting for him there in the person of Colonel George Graham, an officer highly esteemed by the United States government. He had been sent to Campeachy to investigate the privateering establishment. In his report to General Ripley, he says:

Lafitte the Pirate

I reached this place by way of Lake Calcasieu. Such arrangements have been made with General L'Allemande and Mr. Lafitte, who command separate and very distinct establishments here, for the abandonment of the place, as I presume will be entirely satisfactory to the government. It has been promised these gentlemen that in the event of the occupation of this place by the forces of the United States, previous to their departure, they and those under their respective commands shall be protected in their persons and their property. . . . When General Mina was here he commanded a small earthwork about 90 feet square. This work General L'Allemande is finishing. It is situated immediately on the bay, on a ridge which is about three feet higher than the adjacent land, which is, everywhere else within cannon shot, a perfect plain. North and about 400 yards from this work, lies in the bay a large, strong-built brig, about 350 tons burden. She is dismantled, firmly fixed in the sand, and is occupied by Mr. Lafitte as a dwelling, storehouse and arsenal. . . .

When Lafitte found Colonel Graham there, he swallowed his rage and turned a smiling face upon him, assuring him (as usual) that he was violating no laws, that Galveston was not a part of the United States, and that he only conducted his privateering operations against Spanish vessels. Colonel Graham insisted, though, that many Americans believed that Texas had been included in the Louisiana purchase; that the United States and Spain were now friends, and that any depredations against Spanish shipping—even for the cause of Mexican Independence—would be stopped by force of arms if neces-

All Things to All Men

sary. To which, as we see by the letter, Lafitte assented. If the armed forces of the United States came, he would go, he said. But it will be observed that he set no time for his going. Nor did General L'Allemande.

So Graham went away, having delivered his message and having received his answer, while Lafitte remained and continued to function as before. But he was not pleased with the proximity of L'Allemande, for here was a real representative of the Mexican patriots; and Lafitte did not wish to prove his loyalty, despite all his fine promises.

As the inspection by a representative of the government indicates, the officials at Washington were now looking upon Lafitte with suspicious eyes. His reputation was bad and growing worse, and the Spanish minister at Washington was complaining of his constant depredations upon Spanish commerce.

Yet, during all this time, Lafitte was receiving money from the governor of Havana for keeping him posted as to the activities of the anti-Royalist forces.

In the spring of 1819 there assembled at Natchez, a group of citizens whose intention was to aid the Mexican patriots. General Adair was chosen leader, but declined the honor, and second choice fell upon General Long of Virginia. The latter, it is said, pledged his private fortune to the enterprise. In June 1819 his expedition marched to Natchitoches, then to the Sabine River and crossed into

227

Lafitte the Pirate

Texas. His army numbered only four hundred men, but they halted at Nacogdoches and there set up a civil government. Long, as we may surmise, was chosen president. His first act was to issue an invitation to American settlers to come into their new country; Galveston, he assured them, would soon be made a port of entry. Long wrote to Lafitte telling his plans and asking his aid, assuming, of course, that he was working for the Mexican patriots.

Lafitte's answer is characteristic. He promises everything—and nothing. He was anxious to learn Long's plans, and it appears that he was equally anxious to betray them.

Galveston 7 July 1819

Sir:

The letter from you which was delivered to me by Messrs. Johnson and Smith gave me much satisfaction and I hasten to answer it. I will tell you to begin with that I perceive with infinite pleasure your intentions to embrace the cause which I have been upholding for eight years, and which I will never abandon; namely, the emancipation of the Mexican provinces. In accordance with such a profession of faith you cannot really doubt the haste that I shall exercise to unite my efforts with yours. But first I should like to have a more positive understanding.

Since I have entered into this career there have been three major expeditions under the direction of able men, and nevertheless they failed. I helped them with all my means, and I would

All Things to All Men

not regret the sacrifices they have caused me if they had achieved a successful result. But it is true that to-day seems to be a more favorable time, as the state of weakness and exhaustion to which Spain is reduced prevents her from stopping the efforts of these men who desire to be independent. On the other hand they know that through my care in these fertile provinces the growing spirit of liberty is making rapid progress. Now the minds of those young and brave Creoles no longer need to be stimulated, but rather to be directed wisely.

I have been well informed, sir, as to the movements of Arredondo, and I know that he does not have as considerable a force as you think he has. I suppose, however, that it would be well to mistrust him. The agents that I have in San Antonio, assure me that the inhabitants are only waiting for the signal to throw off the yoke. But to help them I need my brother, who is about to arrive from the north, and who will be here in a few days, as I want to have all march at once.

You tell me, sir, that you have hoisted a flag. I please myself in believing, sir, that it is the same one which already exists, for it would be inconvenient to take another than the one for which we have been fighting for eight years; that would show a sort of inconsistency, indecision, and instability, which would only produce a bad effect. Furthermore our flag is recognized at Buenos Aires and Venezuela, and our Corsairs who carry it are received as friends by the authorities of those two provinces. Such is sufficient reason for keeping the colors. As to the establishment of an admiralty court at the port of Galveston, that should have taken place some time ago; but it will be brought about shortly, and the time is not far removed when I shall come to an understanding with you regarding this. As to the munitions of war that you ask of me, I can at present furnish you with but little, as we are awaiting the return of our cruisers in

229

order to fortify ourselves. I will, however, do all that I can for you.

Mr. Johnson tells me that you would like to have an interview with me. That would be as agreeable to me as it would be to you, but it is impossible for me to leave this place; my presence here is absolutely necessary. However, it may be that I shall have that pleasure upon the return of my brother, who will hardly be long in coming.

This, sir, is the situation in which I am placed at present and the disposition in which I find myself. Now let me know exactly what your resources are. Explain to me, I pray you, in the clearest manner the means that you must have to enter into a campaign in order that I may assist you. Indicate to me the course that I should follow in sending to you what I may be able to spare at the time that you are ready to march. Finally, sir, do not allow me to remain in ignorance of anything which will enable me to enter into relations with you, and believe in the high consideration of

Your very humble and Obedient Servant,

JN. LAFITTE

Mr. James Long,
General of the Army of Texas.

We notice that he has lost none of his finesse, nor has he lost his ability for "making phrases." It is probable that Long believed him to be sincere, for as soon as possible he journeyed to Galveston. As a result, L'Allemande's men joined him. Lafitte, however, found excuses. But Long—nothing if not generous—accepted him as a friend, conferred the title of Governor of Galveston upon

All Things to All Men

him, and declared his settlement a Port of Entry to the new Republic of Texas.

How Lafitte repaid him for these favors will be shown in the letter which follows. This letter, marked "Jean Lafitte, Spanish Spy," will be found in the National Archives of Mexico, *Historia, Notas Diplomaticas,* volume four. It is addressed to Juan Manuel de Cagigal, Spanish governor of Havana, Cuba, and it is dated New Orleans, December 11, 1819.

I shall begin, sir, by sending a copy of the letter that I had the honor to write to the Senor Intendent on the seventh of October last, wherein I described the conditions in which matters stand at Galveston. Soon afterwards I learned that he who called himself General Long had found refuge at Galveston with a certain number of Americans, doubtless with the intention of seizing that port. In such circumstances, permit me to say to Your Excellency that it would be well to dispose of those Gentlemen in one way or another. I foresee the most woeful consequences if they take possession, since it is evident that they are the instruments of a Government that seeks means of territorial expansion and that is setting them at work as pioneers. I venture to go so far as to propose to Your Excellency the following plan to dispose of that enemy.

To carry out this plan it is necessary that Your Excellency send to Galveston from eighty to one hundred men under command of a leader who has your confidence, with whom I may work in harmony and whom I shall bring into the port upon recognition by a signal to be agreed upon. I will make it possible for him also to make himself master of the place and to raise the Spanish flag without experiencing any difficulty. As to the

Lafitte the Pirate

objection that the Americans may demonstrate an ardent desire to possess themselves of that port and that they may seek to seize it by such main force as I shall not be able to impede by artifice, I can assure and tranquillize Your Excellency that, with the number of men above mentioned and having a knowledge of the coast in that neighborhood, as I do know it indeed, never, never will the American gentlemen be masters of it.

The time which elapses between these letters is somewhat puzzling until one considers some of the other things which were happening at this period in the pirate's career. His first letter to Long, which was quoted above, was written in July; Long visited him perhaps two months later and Lafitte did not write this letter to the governor of Havana until December, and then from New Orleans. But in the meantime other troubles had come thick and fast.

Lafitte's correspondence with the Spanish officials seems to have been effective, for Long had an unfortunate career after that. His men were attacked and scattered by the army of the Spanish Royalists, and the leader was forced to flee for his life; he crossed the Sabine into Louisiana and did not return to Galveston until 1821.

The buccaneers had plundered so many Spanish vessels that Spain was now wary, and was gradually withdrawing its shipping from the Caribbean and the Mexican Gulf; the merchantmen which sailed nowadays went with strong convoys of armed ships. And, suddenly, pickings became poor for pirates.

All Things to All Men

In addition to loss of revenue, and an actual shortage of worth-while prizes, the bitter realization came to Lafitte that he was losing control of his men. More and more forays upon American vessels were reported, and the buccaneers were not above occasional dangerous onslaughts into Louisiana, where they would steal slaves from one planter and sell them to another. Lafitte was definitely opposed to the latter; not on moral grounds perhaps, but because he knew it to be a dangerous and a petty business; and it was sure to bring disaster, sooner or later.

On October 22, 1819, the Louisiana Courier at New Orleans printed the following notice:

DARING ROBBERY

The house of the subscriber on Bayou Quenede Tortue in the parish of St. Landry was forcibly entered on the night of the 27th of September, by twelve or fourteen armed villains, with their faces blacked (and speaking English), who after tying the undersigned, his wife and children, and threatening to take their lives, if they made any noise or resistance, and under pretence of being officers of government, ransacked the house, and carried off the linen and wearing apparel of the family, together with the following negro slaves, whom a part of these villains had secured, whilst the rest were pillaging the house, viz:

Jack, aged about 50 years, has a bald grey head, foreteeth wanting, his fingers are crooked on one hand, and is about 5 ft. 4 in. high.

Charles, about 12 years old, full face, thick set.

Lafitte the Pirate

Jack, about 12 years old, a scar on one wrist, full forehead and a pointed long chin.

Flora, about 25 years old, a large mole, thick set, and near the time of lying-in.

Phoebe, about 11 years old, thick set, has a scar on her hip.

Neely, about 7 years old, full face, thick set.

Lucy, about 4 years old, full face, thick set.

Anne, about 12 years old, sharp face, slender make.

Susan, about 10 years old, full face, a scar under one eye, thick set.

Jane, about 4 years old, a scar on one side of her head.

Five hundred dollars reward will be given to any person for the recovery of said negro slaves, or fifty dollars each, and a generous reward for the detention and conviction of the robbers.

Parish of St. Landry, October 5th, 1819.

(Signed) JOHN LYONS, Junior

This attack at the plantation house of the Lyons family was so flagrant that the authorities felt obliged to make an effort to apprehend the criminals. The United States navy, which was just beginning to patrol the Gulf for piratical vessels, gave immediate and important assistance. On November 24th the following notice appeared in the Orleans Gazette:

Yesterday a boat of the United States schooner *Lynx* arrived here with four of the men who were concerned in robbing the house of Mr. Lyons, in Attakapas, in the month of September last. It appears that part of the robbers made the best of their

All Things to All Men

way to Galveston, where they were arrested by Jean Lafitte, tried and sentenced to death by a court and jury appointed by Lafitte for that purpose. The leader, George Brown, was hanged in pursuance of the sentence; the rest were pardoned. The Captain of the *Lynx* demanded them when he appeared off Galveston, and they were delivered to him without difficulty.

Lieutenant Commander Madison, of the U. S. S. Lynx, pursued the pirates to Galveston (they had been identified as belonging to Lafitte's settlement) and sent his First Lieutenant, James M. McIntosh, ashore to see Lafitte and to demand that the men be turned over to the United States officers for punishment. Fortunately for us, Lieutenant McIntosh kept a diary, and later wrote an account of his visit to Campeachy. His story was published in the now forgotten Knickerbocker Magazine in March, 1847.

The officer was met by Lafitte with every demonstration of respect, and invited to his dwelling where he presented the written demand of his commander. Lafitte read it and observed: "I am happy that you have succeeded in tracing these vagabonds thus far, and that you will be enabled to identify them by the capture of one of the crew. Assure your commander, Sir, that they will be taken; they cannot now escape me; and it will afford me sincere pleasure to deliver them over to him to be dealt with as pirates. They have acted under no authority from me, nor from any person connected with this government." An officer was sent for, and directed to launch

Lafitte the Pirate

Lafitte's fast-pulling gig, to proceed to the opposite side of the river, and to bring the men to him who had been chased on shore by the boats of the *Lynx*. He then said to Lieutenant McIntosh: "It will be some time in the night before my boat will return, and as you have not more than time to get on board your vessel before dark, and as our bar is a dangerous one to those unacquainted with it, I will not detain you to answer in writing the letter to your commander, but will do so to-morrow when he sends for the men."

Lieutenant McIntosh thanked him for his politeness, took leave, and regained the *Lynx* as night set in; but some considerable danger attended his progress, for a brisk breeze was blowing. The weather prevented his return for five or six days . . . then:

"As the boat neared the low sandy point, it was discovered that a gallows stood there with a body suspended upon it. . . ."

Again the Lieutenant was received with courtesy, and informed that the men were ready, with the exception of the leader, who was hanging on the gallows. "Tell your commander," said Lafitte, "I found the principal of this gang so old an offender, and so very bad a man, that I have saved him the trouble of taking him to the United States. I hung him myself." He now read to Lieutenant McIntosh his communication to the commander of the *Lynx*, who politely asked, before it was sealed, if he might see the letter of Captain Madison to Lafitte, to which this

All Things to All Men

was a reply. After reading it, the Lieutenant said that he regretted, after the kindness and courtesy which he had received from Captain Lafitte and his exertions to procure the men, to decline being the bearer of such a letter to his commander. There were expressions which he deemed discourteous, and threats which would be offensive to that officer. Lafitte quickly replied, that nothing of that kind was intended; and that if Lieutenant McIntosh would be so kind as to point out the offending parts, he would erase them. This was done, the letter copied, read aloud and sealed. Lieutenant McIntosh received it, and departed; not however until Lafitte had advised him not to attempt to cross the bar with his boat so deep as she was, with the additional men, if there was the slightest increase of wind, or if night should overtake him before he reached it.

It was getting late in the afternoon, and the weather was threatening; yet the attempt was made. But night coming on, and finding a rough sea on the bar, it was abandoned, and the boat put about and again headed for the lights of Galveston. Lafitte had anticipated it, and had placed a look-out to report the return of the boat; and on meeting Lieutenant McIntosh, expressed his pleasure at his return. "For," he said, "your boat would have been lost had you attempted to cross the bar with this wind. I hope you will feel perfectly at home with me; your men shall be taken care of, and your prisoners secured until you can make another attempt to get on

Lafitte the Pirate

board." The utmost hospitality was extended to the Lieutenant, and a free and easy conversation took place. Lafitte was asked if he did not sometimes feel himself embarrassed in his position, having around him men of every nation and of all varieties of character, and, as it were, alone in the case of mutiny. He replied: "Never in the least. I understand the management of such men perfectly, and I keep them under good control, as you have just seen, from the prompt manner in which your prisoners have again been ironed, and a sentinel placed over them, by my order. I know precisely how far to go, and I would have saved your commander all trouble in relation to these men if I had dared, for I would have hung every man of them. But I saw, Sir, that to have hung up another would have been the moment to have questioned my power. I made it appear that I considered the example sufficient, and I retained my control."

The next morning nothing could be seen of the *Lynx*. She had during the night again been driven to sea, and a week elapsed before she was again in sight. During this period everything was done to make Lieutenant McIntosh's time pass pleasantly. A fowling-piece with ammunition was at his command; cards and liquor were brought out, and when the hour arrived for his departure the officer felt that he had "passed a week with no common man; with one who, if he had his vices had also his virtues, and who possessed a courteous and gentlemanly deportment seldom equalled and not to be surpassed."

All Things to All Men

This account by young Lieutenant McIntosh seems altogether authentic, as a letter in the archives of the Navy Department verifies his visit. The letter from Lafitte to Lieutenant-Commander Madison is also there, and, even after the offensive language has been stricken out at the young officer's request, the tone remains defiant. Under the date of November 7, 1819, Lafitte says briefly that he is giving up these men because he wants to give them up, not because of threats by the government of the United States, as: "The Port of Galveston belongs to us and is in the possession of the Republic of Texas and was made a Port of Entry the 9th of October last. . . . The Supreme Congress of said republic have thought proper to appoint me governor of this place. . . ."

He was quick enough to take advantage of the title which Long had conferred upon him, even if he did see fit to betray the movements of Long's army to his enemies scarcely thirty days later.

And under "News of the Republic of Texas" in Niles' Weekly Register, we find the following despatch dated from Alexandria, Louisiana, on December 24, 1819:

The *Jupiter* returned to Galveston after a short cruise with a valuable cargo, principally of specie. She is the first vessel that sailed under the authority of Texas. She sailed again on the first inst.

The *Jupiter* was Lafitte's own privateer.

239

Chapter XXIX

THE LAST OF CAMPEACHY

LAFITTE had hanged Brown "as an example to his men," while the *Lynx* was in the offing, and he had talked glibly of the guilt of the others implicated in the Lyons robbery; but as soon as the robbers were in jail in New Orleans, he wrote to his lawyers, Grymes and Livingston, to defend them.

Before these men came to trial, another group of Lafitte's men were caught red-handed. This was about December 1st, 1819.

Lafitte had purchased through his agents in New Orleans, a newly built vessel; and he sent two of his lieutenants, Jean Desfarges and Robert Johnston, with a crew of sixteen men, to bring the purchase to Galveston. On

240

The Last of Campeachy

the homeward voyage, just beyond the mouth of the Mississippi, this pirate crew captured and robbed a vessel; but while they were engaged in looting it, the United States cutter *Alabama* sighted them. The cutter bore down upon the pirates and ordered them to surrender; instead came a volley of gunshot, which cut the *Alabama's* rigging and wounded some of her crew. A sharp engagement followed; Desfarges and Johnston were forced to surrender, and the entire pirate crew was taken in irons to New Orleans.

Upon hearing that his men and his new vessel had been taken, Lafitte hurried to the city to confer with Grymes and Livingston for the defense. With Lafitte's reappearance, many of the old Baratarians flocked to his assistance, and succeeded in working up a sentiment with the rabble in favor of the prisoners. A mob surrounded the rickety old jail and threatened to tear it down. Companies of militia were called out by the Governor and kept guard over the building for several weeks. Balked in this attempt, the mob now threatened to burn the city. The papers were full of news of incendiary fires and other outrages. And the editors denounced these "pirates and bandits" in no uncertain terms. Undeterred by this publicity, unnamed persons succeeded in setting the torch to the State Armory, and burned several buildings in the vicinity of the jail.

Jean Lafitte, needless to say, took no public part in the proceedings; nor did Pierre—who appeared at this time

241

Lafitte the Pirate

in New Orleans, apparently out of nowhere. Instead, both brothers began a fresh protest of their own innocence. Commodore Patterson—the same man who had assisted in destroying Barataria—now stated publicly that there would be no safety on land or sea "until this nest of brigands and murderers at Galveston is broken up."

Pierre Lafitte promptly wrote him a letter, asking for an interview and protesting anew the patriotism of his brother and himself:

New Orleans, January 3, 1820

To Commodore D. F. Patterson, commanding officer of the
New Orleans station:

Sir—

Persuaded that the communication, of which this letter is the object, can conveniently be made to you only; it will, I hope, be received as an apology for the liberty I take of addressing myself to you.

Too long since, the names of the Lafittes have been the object of general execration, as well here as abroad; tarnished and devoted to contempt in publications without any foundation; and always found assimilated and attached to the criminal undertakings of a gang of pirates of all countries, the audacity of which increases by impunity, and who have lately committed depredations and atrocities of all kind on the sea coast, and even within the jurisdiction of this State. It would not be difficult for me to prove that such Banditti never were engaged, kept in pay, or protected by me, or my Brother, in our different transactions at Galveztown; and his late conduct in that country, with regard to one of them, ought to destroy the least suspi-

The Last of Campeachy

cion. But, as the non-ratification of the treaty by Spain gives to the government of the United States the jurisdiction as far west as the Rio Bravo del Norte under the purchase of Louisiana; and as the establishment at Galveztown, lying within those limits, was formed as conquered from Spain, by the Mexican Republic, and Republic of Texas; to put an end to all things, and to show to the whole world that I never contributed to the violation of the sacred rights of nations, or would offer resistance or offence to the Government of the United States; and in the view of restoring all confidence to the foreign trade directing itself towards this place; and to destroy all fears which the establishment of Galveztown might occasion: I now offer myself to you, Sir, willingly, and at my own risk and expense, to clear Galveztown, and disband all those which are to be found there; taking the engagement for myself and my Brother, that it shall never serve as a place of Rendezvous for any undertakings with our consent, or under our authorization. If the offer I make to you, Sir, can receive your approbation, I shall stand in need of no other thing but the necessary permit to prevent any embarassment in the enterprize, offering at the same time any satisfactory security for its unforeseen results, with permission to all those to be found there to retire where they may choose.

If my demand is accepted, nothing shall be wanted on my part, to bring it to a good result; and if you contribute to the general welfare by securing the Commerce and inhabitants against the audacious attempts of Ruffians; I shall be indebted to you, Sir, for giving me the opportunity of striking out the odious epithets affixed to my name by my enemies; and of evincing to the Government of the United States my earnest desire to comply with the Laws; and as far as may be in my power to conduce to the safety of the Commerce of this Port, and ridding the Gulf of Mexico of Cruizers obnoxious to the Government.

I remain, Sir, your most humble and obedient Servant.

PIERRE LAFITTE

P. S.   In case you take the present in consideration, I beg leave to call on you, on the day you may be pleased to appoint.

Commodore Patterson appears to have paid no more attention to this letter than he had paid to those other protestations of innocence back in the days before Barataria was destroyed. But this is the last real record concerning Pierre Lafitte. Afterwards, he disappears, and there is only an unverified fragment concerning his later life.

Soon the pirates were brought to the United States District Court, tried and convicted. Despite the pleas of their able attorneys, the men were sentenced to hang.

On hearing the result, Jean Lafitte, armed with letters and recommendations from influential merchants and politicians, hastened to Washington to see the President. What happened there is difficult to find out at this late date, but the men were reprieved for sixty days, and one of them was freed. Desfarges and Johnston, however, were hanged at the foot of Saint Ann Street, from the yard-arm of one of the United States cruisers anchored in the Mississippi. On May 26th, 1820, the Courier prints the following notice:

The Last of Campeachy

Jean Desfarges and Robert Johnston, the former captain, and the latter lieutenant of the schooner captured some time since by Captain Loomis, who had been found guilty of piracy, were executed yesterday at twelve o'clock. Out of the sixteen other men who composed the crew of that vessel, only one has been pardoned by the President of the United States. His name is John Tuckers. He had been recommended to mercy by the jury. The others have been reprieved for 60 days from the 25th inst.

The remaining pirates were, however, not executed until well along in the following year. And a controversy concerning them raged in the newspapers—a controversy which did not concern their guilt or innocence, but which, oddly enough, related to the expense of keeping them alive for so long a time in the prison at New Orleans. One newspaper editor has figured out the expenses of such reprieves and announces editorially that the long delay has cost the city $27,375 already.

The newspapers now demand that "this viper's brood at Galveston must be destroyed."

Despite all his protestations, Jean Lafitte's prestige was gone.

He went back to Galveston, and his vessels continued to sail into the Gulf and the Caribbean as before. But his men were unruly; there were quarrels, thefts and mutinies. Worse, an American vessel had been taken by one of his cruisers, plundered, and then scuttled at Matagorda. The United States sent Messrs. Davis and John-

Lafitte the Pirate

son and Dr. Oliver from New Orleans to investigate the affair, and their report was unfavorable to Lafitte.

There were numerous desertions, as attested by the following notice in Niles' Register:

New Orleans, Nov. 21, 1820. We learn that Jacques Lacroix and James Louis Rouey have been pardoned by the President of the United States. These men were convicted before the district court of the United States for this district at the last July term, of a piracy committed in May last on a Spanish vessel called the *Constitution*, bound from Vera Cruz to Tampico. Their vessel belonged to the squadron of Jean Lafitte. It appeared on the trial that they were deceived in regard to the objects of the cruise they had undertaken, and that as soon as they discovered the real character of their officers, they denounced them to the crew, and endeavored to make their escape. For these reasons the jury unanimously recommended them to mercy, which recommendation, we understand, was urged upon the president by Judge Hall, confirmed by his own solicitations.

Lafitte was forty years old, and his black hair was growing gray. His old trick of closing one eyelid was now carried to such an extent that many believed him to be blind in one eye. He was morose and shabby; and, like so many other broken-hearted men, he had grown fat. He seldom mingled with his men, but sat alone and in silence.

But he had not lost his ability to make fine phrases.

Summoned by the United States to produce the national authority by which he occupied the harbor of Gal-

The Last of Campeachy

veston, he answered that he had found the port abandoned, and had taken possession of it with the idea of preserving and maintaining it at his own cost. Then he makes one of his ever-surprising patriotic statements:

In so doing I was satisfying the two passions which imperiously dominate in me; that of offering an asylum to the armed vessels of the party of independence, and of placing myself in position (considering its proximity to the United States) to fly to their assistance should circumstances demand it. . . . I know, Sir, that I have been calumniated in the vilest manner by persons invested with certain authority, but, fortified by a conscience which is irreproachable in every respect, my internal tranquility has not been affected, and, in spite of my enemies, I shall obtain the justice due me.

But the government was not impressed. The depredations upon American citizens, and the general piratical tenor of Lafitte's occupation, with complaints from the Spanish and American governments, induced the authorities to send to Galveston, early in 1821, Lieutenant Kearny, in the United States brig-of-war, *Enterprize.* Lafitte went out over the bar to meet him, and escorted him ashore. The entertainment was lavish, the wines delightful and the host most cordial; but this did not deter Kearny from delivering his message: The government of the United States commanded Lafitte to abandon Galveston.

There was no alternative. Lafitte shrugged his shoul-

Lafitte the Pirate

ders and accepted his fate. He had played his game and lost; now he was ready to go.

He asked for two months in which to wind up his affairs, and Kearny assented, stating however, that he must return to the island at the time of Lafitte's departure. This was necessary, he pointed out, as he must assure his government that Lafitte had gone.

And so it was arranged.

In those two months, Lafitte settled with his lieutenants and his men; some of them wished to go with their chief; others to return to New Orleans, and he arranged for their passage; still others wished to settle on the mainland in Texas. He agreed to all their wishes with but one stipulation: they must leave Campeachy. He had decided to destroy the settlement completely; nothing should remain. The island would be left again to the wild creatures, the sea-gulls, the terns and the pelicans.

A young officer who accompanied Kearny on that last visit to Lafitte, wrote an account of it afterwards. It is such a pleasant picture that I shall quote part of it here. The excerpt is from a longer report in the United States Magazine and Democratic Review for July, 1839. It begins with a description of the approach to Galveston, and of locating the fleet as it lay in the harbor, ready to sail:

The brig lay at anchor right ahead of us. She was a vessel of about two hundred tons and sixteen guns, a pretty model and apparently ready for sea. Not far from her lay a long,

248

MASPERO'S EXCHANGE COFFEE HOUSE

THE RUINS OF FORT LIVINGSTON

The Last of Campeachy

black, clipper-built schooner, with low black hull and lofty fish-ing-rods of masts, the very beau-ideal of a pirate.

We pulled first to the brig—she was full of men; all sorts of faces, white, yellow, black and dingy, in caps, sombreros, Mexican hats, with every variety of expression, reconnoitered us from the bulwarks and ports, and seemed to look with but little love at the cocked hat and epaulettes of the regular man-of-war.

"Is Captain Lafitte on board?"

"No, *Signor*," a hardy-looking, grey-headed old fellow answered, taking his *cigana* from his mouth and proceeding to light a fresh one. He gave us some direction in Spanish which I did not understand; the extent of which was, however, that *Il Capitano* might be found on board the schooner; and to the schooner we rowed accordingly. To our enquiry Captain La-fitte answered himself, with an invitation to come on board.

My description of this renowned chieftain, to correspond with the original, will shock the preconceived notions of many who have hitherto pictured him as the hero of a novel or a melodrama. I am compelled by truth to introduce him as a stout, rather gentlemanly personage, some five feet ten inches in height, dressed very simply in a foraging cap and blue frock coat of a most villainous fit; his complexion, like most Creoles, olive; his countenance full, mild, and rather impressive, but for a small black eye, which now and then, as he grew animated in conversation, would flash in a way which impressed me with a notion that *Il Capitano* might be when roused, a very ugly customer.

His demeanor toward us was exceedingly courteous; and, upon learning Captain Kearny's mission, he invited us below, and tendered, to use an aldermanlike phraze, "the hospitalities of the vessel"; and here, while I recall the flavor of that shrub

Lafitte the Pirate

and water, I will observe, that I once heard from the lips of an experienced sea-dog. "It is not at all wonderful that so many embrace the calling of a buccaneer, when one has an opportunity of witnessing the manner of life which these rovers lead. Instead of four-water-grog, salt junk and pork soup; your free traders of Cape Antonio will mess upon all the luxuries of life —real chateau, burgundy, West India preserves and real havanas, *ad libitum*. The spoils of all nations are enjoyed and squandered with reckless profusion. Free license for all indulgences, and the influence of a never-failing summer, tempt the idle and dissolute with pleasure unbought, and luxury without toil; and the strictest discipline is needed on board vessels stationed in those seas, to guard a crew from the enervating and corrupting tendency of climate and example."

"I am making my arrangements," Lafitte observed, "to leave the bay. The ballast of the brig has been shifted. As soon as we can get her over the bar, Captain, we sail."

"We supposed that your flotilla was larger," Captain Kearny remarked.

"I have men on shore," said Lafitte—not apparently noticing the remark, "who are destroying the fort, and preparing some spars for the brig. Will you go on shore and look at what I am doing?"

All this was said with the slightest possible accent. Our skipper assenting to the proposal.

We returned to the deck, and Lafitte pointed us to the preparations which had been made on board the brig for getting her to sea. The schooner on board which we were mounted a long gun amidships, and some six nine-pounders a side. There were, I should think, fifteen or twenty men on deck, apparently of all nations, and below I could observe there were a great many more. There was no appearance of any uniform among

The Last of Campeachy

them, nor, to the eye of a man-of-war's man, much discipline. The officers, or those who appeared such, were in plain clothes, and Lafitte himself was without any distinguishing mark of his rank. Having ordered his boat he pushed off, and we followed.

Landing, as before, on a white sandy beach, beyond which we had the uninteresting prospect of a flat extent of country, diversified with a stub growth of cedar, and black, stagnant-looking bayous. It was a desolate looking place.

On the shore, we passed a long shed under which a party were at work, and round which junk, cordage, sails, and all sorts of heterogeneous matters were scattered in confusion. Beyond this we came across a four-gun fort. It had been advantageously located, and was a substantial looking affair, but now was nearly dismantled, and a gang were completing the work of destruction. I observed a number of English or Americans among the men at work; their fair complexions, although embrowned by constant exposure, contrasting strongly with the swarthy visages of the Spanish and French.

"You see, Captain, I am getting ready to leave; I am friendly to your country, Captain; I know New Orleans well; I have good friends there. Ah," continued he, shaking his head significantly, "they call me a pirate, but I might have done them some good service when I lay at Barataria. But I am not a pirate. You see there?" said he, pointing suddenly toward the point of the beach.

"I see," said our skipper; "what does that mean?"

The object to which our attention was thus directed, and which we had previously observed with anything but admiration, was the dead body of a man dangling from a rude gibbet erected on the beach.

"That is my justice. That villain plundered an American

251

Lafitte the Pirate

schooner. The captain complained to me of him, and he was found guilty, and hung."

"These look like graves," said Captain Kearny, pointing to two equivocal looking hillocks in the sand.

"Yes, that was a terrible villain; he was caught in a plan to murder my steward, who then had in his hands almost all my people's money; we gave him court-martial fairly, and he was sentenced to be shot by the steward, and so he was. A very great villain. Will you go on board my brig?"

On board this vessel there was evidently a greater attention paid to discipline. Lafitte led the way into his cabin, where preparation had already been made for dinner; to partake which we were frankly invited, and which invitation (I can answer for one) most willingly accepted. Sea air and exercise are proverbial persuaders of the appetite; and Monsieur Lafitte's display of good stew, dried fish and wild turkey, cured in the sun, as he told us, were more tempting than prize money— that is, just at that time. There was, however, a surprise in store for us that, hungry as we were, made us almost oblivious to our dinner. Forth, from a state room, issued a lady—one of the most glorious specimens of the brunette ever dreamed of. A full and voluptuous form of faultless outline, beautiful features, and sleepy black eyes, with the blackest and most luxuriant hair that ever curled; her beauty was enough to drive a squad of sentimental youths like ourselves to poetry or suicide.

She was evidently a quadroon; and, as Lafitte did not introduce us, we did what our timidity could; and, taking advantage of a rather courteous gesture in answer to a proffer of some boiled yam, I commenced an acquaintance by some apt remark, the precise context of which I have forgotten, and, judging from her manner, should have acquired some footing in her good graces, had she understood my vernacular, which,

The Last of Campeachy

alas! she did not. Our intercourse, therefore, was carried on through the medium of signs, and limited to reciprocities in Turkey and French wine. Meanwhile M'Kenny had remarked to Lafitte of our visit to Matagorda. He listened with attention, and answered briskly: "It is lucky you did not meet the Indians; they are Camanches; I know them; those very fellows killed and ate two of my men."

"Ate?" said I.

"Yes, ate; they are cannibals; stay while I tell you; I send one of my people one day there to hunt; in the evening he does not come back; next day I send more to look for him, but nobody finds him; I think then that he has fallen into some pit, or has run away; some days afterwards two more of my men go to hunt; in the evening they are missing; then I do not know what to think; I take a party and search everywhere, but find nothing of them; as we return we hear a shout; we return it, thinking it may be our people; directly we hear another shout, and we see a man running for his life to us, and half a hundred of the devils after him; when they saw us they stopped, and in a moment they all vanished; when the man came to us it was Juan Perez, our carpenter; he was so frightened and breathless at first that he could not speak, but presently he told us; that the Indians had killed the man who went out first, and ate him; and Perez, with his companion, had been also captured; that very day they were to have been a feast for the savage villains, and one of them had been knocked in the head; Perez had slipped his hands from the rope which confined him, and ran for life, and, lucky for him, we were near enough to save him; I afterwards took as many men as we wanted for safety, and went to the place from which Perez escaped; the Indians had gone but we saw the remains of their fire, and the blackened bones of their victims; I assure you there is no doubt."

The quadroon had been, during this time, flirting dreadfully with our Mid, as far as dividing oranges into quarters and drinking silent healths could go. All at once she placed the glass, which she was raising to her lips, on the table, and, rising hastily, left us without further leave-taking. Glancing my eye at Lafitte, I intercepted one single look of that black eye directed towards her, so concentrated and severe in its meaning, that I did not wonder that it frightened the poor girl away from the table.

We afterwards became quite sociable, under the influence of the most generous and racy wines, honestly come by, no doubt, all except the skipper, who kept a bright look out upon all that was going forward, and allowed us, I suppose, to be as communicative as we pleased, in the hope of hearing something in return which might be useful to Government.

Meanwhile our conversation ran into the various topics which a sailor's experience can suggest, and Lafitte spoke unreservedly of his hazardous and adventurous life. He was evidently educated and gifted with no common talent for conversation; and, while listening to many a tale of shipwreck and storm, peril and daring, it seemed to me that I had realized some of the romances which had whiled my school days, and had heard from his own lips the exploits of one of the sea kings. "Come gentlemen," at length Lafitte observed, after a pause, at the end of a thrilling story. "You do not like my wine;—Fernan," (speaking to the steward) "Café."

"I should like very much to hear your life, Captain," I remarked.

He smiled, and shrugged his shoulders, "It is nothing extraordinary," said he. "I can tell it in a very few words. But

The Last of Campeachy

there was a time," and he drew a long breath, "when I could not tell it without cocking both pistols. Bah! I'll tell you my life.

"Eighteen years ago I was a merchant in San Domingo. My father before me, was a merchant. I had become rich. I had married a wife. She was rich and beautiful," he stifled a sigh, and went on, "I determined to go to Europe, and I wound up all my affairs in the West Indies. I sold my property there. I bought a ship, and loaded her, besides which, I had on board a large amount of specie, all that I was worth, in short. Well, Sir, when the vessel that I was aboard had been a week at sea, we were overhauled by a Spanish man-of-war, commanded by Senhor Chevalier D'Alkala. Yes, I remember his name, for I settled my debt with him afterwards, at any rate," he continued, with a thoughtful kind of chuckle. "The Spaniards captured us. They took every thing—goods, specie, even my wife's jewels. They set us on shore upon a barren sand key, with just provisions enough to keep us alive a few days, until an American schooner took us off, and landed us in New Orleans. I did not care what became of me. I was a beggar. My wife took the fever from exposure and hardship, and died in three days after my arrival. I met some daring fellows, who were as poor as I was. We bought a schooner, and declared against Spain eternal war! Fifteen years I have carried on a war against Spain. So long as I live I am at war with Spain, but no other nation. I am at peace with the world, except Spain. Although they call me a pirate, I am not guilty of attacking any vessel of the English or French. I showed you the place where my own people had been punished for plundering American property. At New Orleans I refused to be the enemy of America. Captain, will you take coffee?"

This ceremony over, we went on deck, and made our adieu

Lafitte the Pirate

to the gallant rover. The fair—no, not the fair, but the beautiful quadroon did not re-appear. With feelings far more interested for the gallant rover than either would have chosen to confess, we shook hands, as for the last time in this world; and . . . rowed back to the brig.

The next night Lafitte burned Galveston.

Sailors aboard the *Enterprize* saw the settlement burst into flames, and watched the dry, wooden houses burn like straw. Soon the town was but a flaring torch. As the shadows receded the whole harbor was visible.

The pirate's fleet was gone.

Turning, the sailors saw three vessels beyond the harbor bar. They seemed suspended in space between black water and blacker sky; their flowing sails were red in the firelight. Silently they moved before the wind on their unhurried way. There was no signal and no farewell. For a time the sails gleamed ruddily against the dark; then, one by one, they faded and were gone. Out of the firelight, into a dark sea. . . .

Out of life, into dim legend.

Chapter XXX

FRAGMENTS

HISTORIANS disagree concerning the date of Jean Lafitte's departure from Galveston; some writers assert that he left the island as early as May 12th, 1820, while others give various dates in 1821. William Bollaert, one of the most painstaking and accurate chroniclers of the buccaneer's history, speaks of the exodus as taking place "on an unnamed day, early in 1821." And I am inclined to agree with him.

With the disappearance of the pirate fleet into the dark, the history of Lafitte comes to an end. Beyond that there are only fragments, brief notices in the newspapers of the period—and a mass of contradictory and improbable legends. It is evident that Lafitte's talents lay in or-

Lafitte the Pirate

ganization and management, rather than in piratical warfare; but, with his establishment broken up, and his men scattered, we find him engaged in actual piracy, which he seems to have bungled rather badly. Each public outcry against him adds another declining note in the pirate's swan song.

The Courier for March 19th, 1821, gives the following communication from Charleston, South Carolina:

We understand that a schooner called the *Nancy Eleanor*, on board of which was Pierre Lafitte, brother of the celebrated pirate of that name, left this port in a clandestine manner a few nights since. It is said she had on board arms and a large number of men, and is supposed to be bound on a piratical expedition.

This was at the approximate time that Jean Lafitte was driven from Galveston. Did the brothers meet, one wonders, to join forces somewhere in the Caribbean or in the Mexican Gulf? It appears so, for in Niles' Register for December 22nd, 1821, we find the following combination despatch from Cuba:

The official account of the capture of a piratical vessel was published at Havana. The whole crew of the picaroon was either killed or wounded, with the exception of the famous pirate Lafitte and three others, who escaped in the boat at the moment of boarding. At the same time, two prizes of the pirate were re-captured, together with some negroes, which had fallen into the hands of these plundering villains.

The rains are so excessive as to greatly injure the crops,

Fragments

and nearly prevent communication with the interior. The custom-house at Havana closed five days, in consequence of the excessive fall of it.

The brig *Belvedere,* commanded by Captain Lamson, arrived at the New Orleans levee in May, 1822, with the news that the vessel had been attacked by pirates in the Gulf. The log of the vessel was printed in the Courier on May 22nd, and it gives a long account of an unsuccessful attempt by pirates to capture the brig. But in the latter part of the record there is something which is of more interest to us:

Spoke the U. S. schooner *Allegator* [wrote Captain Lamson], under Lieutenant-Commander Stockton, off Sugar Key, coast of Cuba; was informed on board that they had burnt a schooner, taken another and sloop from the pirates, and an English brig, the captain and mate having been hung by them. The *Allegator* also had retaken the Columbian schooner *Sinega* from her crew who had mutinied and run away with her. When the *Belvedere* parted from the *Allegator,* Captain Stockton was inshore with a schooner of light draught of water, with 70 men, belonging to the *Grampus* and *Allegator,* together with the three crews of the prizes which he had taken, when they commenced exchanging shots with a piratical schooner of 70 men, but being very much crowded it was very doubtful if he could take her. The famous Lafitte was amongst them.

This chance bit of information connects Lafitte directly with piracy on the open seas and with armed opposition to the forces of the United States.

259

Lafitte the Pirate

In the Louisiana Advertiser we find an account of the capture by pirates of the ship *Orleans*. No names are given, but the pirate chief, upon leaving with his spoils, sent this note to the captain:

> At sea and in good luck.
>
> Sir:
>
> Between buccaneers, no ceremony. I take your dry goods and in return I send you a pimento; there, we are now even; I entertain no resentment.
>
> Bid good day to the officer of the United States and tell him I appreciate the energy with which he has spoken of me and my companions in arms. Nothing can intimidate us; we share the same hazards, and our maxim is: "That the goods of the world belong to the strong and valiant."
>
> The occupation of the Floridas is a pledge that the course I follow is in conformity with the policy now pursued by the United States.
>
> (Signed) RICHARD COEUR DE LION

The Creoles read the story and smiled grimly: "That's that Lafitte!" they said. But there was no proof of it.

The last bit of information is from an editorial in the Courier for November 29th, 1822:

> We have been informed that the famous Lafitte of piratical memory, after having been wrecked on the island of Cuba, being destitute of all means of living, and of escape, had been discovered and apprehended by some inhabitants, who brought him to Porto Principe, where he was thrown into a dungeon. Unfortunately for mankind, Lafitte was recognized by several

Fragments

influential persons of the place, to whom he had formerly rendered some service, and who facilitated his escape. We cannot avoid applauding the feeling of gratitude which moved these persons to break the chains of their benefactor, but at the same time we cannot too deeply regret that the monster who has shed so much innocent blood, should have, perhaps for the hundredth time, escaped the sword of Justice, which has so long been hanging over his guilty head.

If the editor of the Courier was correctly informed, then Jean Lafitte has fallen into evil times indeed. Only seven years before he had been the hero of New Orleans. . . .

There were other piratical vessels in the Gulf, and the newspaper stories of robbery and murder at sea are numerous, but like so much of the journalism of that day, the accounts are incomplete and the names of few pirates are given, even in captures. By 1823 the United States and England had united forces in driving the pirates from the Gulf. We read of many captures and of some hard fighting. On May 12th, the Courier prints a notice that Commodore Porter's squadron has captured four pirate vessels and all their prizes and "had nearly destroyed all the pirates in the West India seas."

By 1825, the day of the buccaneer was over. The Latin-American States had established their independence and this had put an end to the issuance of privateering licenses. It was piracy now; no longer could any stretch of the imagination call it privateering; and pirates were

Lafitte the Pirate

hanged. Armed government cruisers patrolled the Gulf, and at last the danger of sea travel was reduced to the hazard of wind and wave.

Yoakum, the Texas historian, believes that Jean Lafitte died of fever and was buried at Silan, Yucatan, in 1826. If we examine his source material we find that he bases his conclusion upon three letters. One of these is from Thomas M. Duke to Ferdinand Pinckard Esq., at Galveston; the date is May 1843. Mr. Duke says:

In answer to your letter, I have to state that Lafitte, the celebrated pirate, died in Yucatan, at an Indian town named Silan, about fifteen miles from Merida. He died in the second year of the independence of Mexico (1826) and was buried in the Campo Santo of Silan. A tombstone was placed over him, stating his name, age and time of his death,—which is not now recollected by me. The same statement was made to me by the old Portuguese named Manuel Lopez, who served with him in Barataria, and sailed under him from Charleston, South Carolina, for the island of Los Mugeres near the coast of Yucatan. Lafitte then loaded the vessel with salt and dye woods and sent it back to Charleston, and accompanied by Lopez crossed over in a fishing boat to Silan, where he took sick and died. Lopez assisted in burying him. . . . This account is corroborated by many who were there with Commodore Thompson and Captain Boylan, during the Texas cruise in 1837. The late Judge Rhoades and several others stated to me the same facts. . . .

Two letters from Judge Rhoades are among the

Fragments

papers of Mirabeau Bounaparte Lamar in the Texas State Library. He wrote to Lamar in 1838:

At the island of Mugeres off the coast of Yucatan . . . I became acquainted with an old turtle fisher called Gregorio. In speaking of the trade of these islands and the character of the traders, the name of Captain Lafitte was introduced; he said he knew him well, that he had often been there, and that once he (Gregorio) went with him to Galveston Island. He spoke of him in high terms, and observed that he helped bury him . . . that he died of fever and was buried in the neighborhood.

In his second letter, Judge Rhoades says that he has found notes made at the time of his visit to Mugeres, and supplements his information with this:

Lafitte died at Losbocas, 59 leagues from Campeachy on the north coast of Yucatan, and was buried at Silan, two leagues from Losbocas. This I had from an old half-Mexican, half-indian named Gregorio, who had been a prisoner with him, and had been to Galveston Island. He died of fever.

This evidence is far from conclusive, but it is the best we have.

Those who have followed the history of Jean Lafitte so far may be interested to know what became of those other men and women who have played a part in these pages. And I shall try to tell you, briefly.

Lafitte the Pirate

Of Pierre Lafitte, I can find nothing after the notice from the Courier printed earlier in this chapter; but it is evident that he visited New Orleans as late as 1824, as the last child born to him and Marie Louise Villars was baptised in the Church of Saint Louis early in 1825.

His son, Pierre the younger, of whom we caught a brief glimpse in the beginning of this volume, grew to manhood in the home of the Sauvinets, married Marie Berret, a native of Cuba, and left descendants in New Orleans. His first son, François, was born on August 23rd, 1828. The New Orleans directory for 1830 shows that he was living with his wife at 67 Barracks Street.

Of Adelaide Maselari, I can find nothing; but her daughter Marie Josephe Lafitte was living with the Sauvinets at 141 Hospital Street in 1830. She was then twenty years old and unmarried. Whether she left descendants or not, I have not been able to find out.

Of Pierre, the son of Jean Lafitte and Catherine Villars, I can find no trace. But the seven children of Pierre, the elder, and Marie Louise Villars the quadroon grew to maturity. The oldest daughter, Rose, passed for a white woman, married a white man and had several children. This fact was brought out in a lawsuit in 1920.

In that year a man in New Orleans (I shall give no names) married a granddaughter of Rose Lafitte. Shortly after he sued for an annulment of the marriage on the grounds that his wife was of colored blood. The bitter legal controversy which followed dragged on for

264

Fragments

two years, involving a suit against the New Orleans
Board of Health to have the records changed in the city's
books. On November 20th, 1922, Judge Wayne G. Rogers
of the Civil District Court refused to change the records
from "Negro" to "White." This automatically annulled
the marriage, for the Louisiana Law is specific:

> A marriage between persons of white and colored races is
> prohibited in this State, as a matter of public order and policy,
> and such a contract is absolutely null, requires no direct action
> to set it aside, and may be attacked by the party to whom it is
> opposed, by way of exception or defence, whenever and where-
> ever it is set up.

In compiling the material for this book, I stumbled
upon a mention of this lawsuit. Mr. Henry Lanause of
the New Orleans Board of Health permitted me to read
the hundreds of typewritten pages of court record; and
while this record gave me little direct information, it gave
a clue to other fields for investigation. And it was in this
way that I managed to learn the story of Jean Lafitte and
Catherine Villars, as handed down for four generations.
It also led to the records in the archives of the Saint Louis
Cathedral.

To turn now to the other men and women who have
wandered in and out of these pages:

Andrew Jackson, as every one knows, became president of the United States; and when this honor came to
him, he did not forget his friends in New Orleans. Ed-

Lafitte the Pirate

ward Livingston succeeded Martin Van Buren as Secretary of State in Jackson's Cabinet in 1831; two years later he was made Minister to France, as his brother had been before him. He died in 1836, leaving an international reputation as a lawyer. His memory was preserved in Louisiana in several ways; a Parish was given his name, and in 1841 a fort built at Grande Terre was named for him. Oddly enough—or suitably enough—the fort stands where Lafitte's slave barracoon stood, more than a century ago. Fort Livingston was partially destroyed by a tropical hurricane which swept Barataria in 1893, and after that it was abandoned; but the high, somber walls remain, surmounted by broken cannon. And the ruined fort still keeps guard over the ruins of the pirate's kingdom.

William Charles Cole Claiborne, having served as governor of Louisiana from 1804 until 1817, retired from the governorship and was elected to the United States Senate. He died in the same year, and his widow— "the most beautiful, fascinating and coquettish woman in New Orleans"—married none other that Mr. John Randolph Grymes.

And Grymes remained throughout his lifetime the same full-blooded gentleman that we have seen in his earlier days. He was elected to the Louisiana Legislature, and fought two duels over hot words in the House of Representatives. In 1845 he was a delegate to the Constitutional Convention, and later became United States

Fragments

District Attorney. He died in 1854. Once, in his later life, the opposing attorney in a case before the Supreme Court, made a violent personal attack upon his manners and morals during the course of a trial, hoping, it is said, to divert Grymes from the evidence in hand. He listened patiently, and showed no displeasure. When the young man had finished his tirade, Grymes addressed the Court: "Your Honors, I have not experienced a passion, or entertained an emotion in more than twenty years." Then he continued with his argument and won the case. This characteristic comment has become a classic of the Louisiana Bar.

General Humbert, who behaved so badly at his birthday dinner, and so well at the Battle of New Orleans, could not resist the lure of the Mexican patriots. He enlisted in New Orleans in 1816, about one thousand men, the first and largest filibustering expedition that ever marched out of the city. With his men he fought his way into the very heart of Mexico, reenforced by the Indian chief Toledo. But the backbone of the revolution had been broken before he arrived, and although he won some small victories over the Royalist forces, he at last yielded to the inevitable, and disbanding his army in 1817, he returned to New Orleans. All that we know of his later life is that he taught "in a French college"—presumably Orleans College, and until the very end of his career, he was one of the best customers at taverns of New Orleans. He died

Lafitte the Pirate

in February, 1823. His grave is unmarked and forgotten.

Gambi, the most ferocious and bloodthirsty of Lafitte's buccaneers, was murdered by his own men.

Chighizola, or Nez Coupé, ended more peacefully. In his later years he sold fruit in the French market working in partnership with John B. Lorenzo, a boy whom he had befriended in Barataria, and who later became a successful commission merchant in New Orleans. Chighizola swaggered until the last, and was never happier than when telling of his piratical exploits and of his miraculous reformation. Many of his descendants live to-day on Grande Isle.

Beluche had a more distinguished career. Andrew Jackson had been impressed with his skill at the Battle of New Orleans and gave him a written recommendation for bravery. Armed with this, Beluche went to Venezuela and later to Colombia, where he became a commodore in the navy, and sailed the sea until he died.

Of all Lafitte's lieutenants, Dominique You proved the most popular. He settled in New Orleans, where he was highly esteemed. He came into prominence at the time of the plot to rescue Napoleon from St. Helena. Briefly, it was like this:

A certain Captain Bossiere owned a swift clipper-schooner called the *Seraphine,* and he planned to go with a small group of picked men to the island where Napoleon was a prisoner, kidnap him and bring him to New Orleans to spend his declining years among his friends and ad-

THE GRAVE OF DOMINIQUE YOU

HOTEL AT LAST ISLAND,
DESTROYED BY A HURRICANE

Fragments

mirers. Napoleon, it is said, had expressed a wish to come to America. Nicholas Girod, the millionaire-mayor of New Orleans, financed the expedition. He went further, and prepared a house for Napoleon. Concerning this house there is some debate: some claim that Napoleon was to share Girod's palatial residence which still stands to-day, just opposite Maspero's Exchange Coffee House; others say that Girod intended giving him another house, nearby in Chartres Street. It really does not matter, as Napoleon never saw either of them. But the plot went on apace, and Dominique You was one of the leaders of the party.

Three days before the departure of the *Seraphine,* the news of Napoleon's death on May 5th, 1821, reached New Orleans.

After that Dominique devoted himself to a peaceful life, and became a popular figure in the city. "It may seem superfluous to add," says George W. Cable, "that he became a leader in ward politics."

He was open-handed and generous, but he died in abject poverty on November 15th, 1830, too proud, even in his last illness, to ask for help. He was buried at the expense of the town council, and laid to rest with full military honors. His tomb stands on the central aisle in Saint Louis Cemetery Number Two, not far from the place where Pierre Lafitte, the younger, is buried. The tablet on Dominique You's tomb bears the emblem of Free Masonry, and below is an epitaph, in French and

Lafitte the Pirate

in verse, which proclaims him "the intrepid hero of a hundred battles on land and sea; who, without fear and without reproach, will one day view, unmoved, the destruction of the world."

Chapter *XXXI*

THE LEGENDARY LAFITTE

AMUSINGLY enough, Lord Byron is responsible for the beginning of the Lafitte legend. Reading an account of the Battle of New Orleans, the poet was pleased with the pirate who turned patriot. In 1816, he wrote a poem called "The Corsair." It is the tale of a fictitious hero who resembles the Baratarian not at all; nor did Byron try to give a picture of the man. But, as a foot-note to the poem, a clipping from an American newspaper pertaining to Lafitte's career is given. This was enough for the Victorian writers who followed. They licked their chops before the combination of Byron and Lafitte; and the jingle at the end of the poem pleased them immoderately:

Lafitte the Pirate

He left a corsair's name to other times,
Linked with one virtue and a thousand crimes.

Every sentimentalist who has written about Lafitte—
and, Lord help us! there have been enough—has quoted
that couplet. The writers did not trouble themselves with
the poem itself, nor with documents of any kind; they
merely copied each other's stories, always amplifying
them to suit themselves. As an example, there is the story
of Claiborne's offer of a reward for the pirate's capture,
and of Lafitte's jest by offering a larger reward for the
governor's arrest. Many articles concerning the pirate
use this story, and each time it is repeated, the reward
grows larger. I shall quote only one, but it will suffice:
"Governor Claiborne offered a reward of five thousand
dollars for the pirate's *head* (Tut, tut!) and the brave
buccaneer immediately offered a reward of fifty thousand
dollars for the head of the governor!" If this had been
the case it is likely that Claiborne would have been de-
capitated by some hard-up Baratarian.

In 1831, only six years after Lafitte's disappearance,
the Casket, a magazine for young ladies, published a romance called "The Baratarian Chief, or, Lafitte." There
was a subtitle which stated that the story was "founded
on fact." This is the beginning of the "redemption
through love of a noble woman" motif. Lafitte is pictured
as a dashing young fellow, misunderstood by the authorities; but he has a heart of gold beneath his piratical ex-

The Legendary Lafitte

terior. The tale is full of such expressions as "Zounds!" and "Mayhap 'tis true." The hero is saved by his love for a pure, beautiful blond called Mary Mornton of Charleston (or Savannah); he marries her and reforms. It is the type of story in which the author proves that he is a great writer by sheer elegance of style. If, for example, a girl with blue eyes puts her head out of a window, some one exclaims: "I perceive a fair female form at yon casement! Her lustrous orbs of azure stir my soul, etc. . . ."

I mention this trivial tale only because subsequent writers of so-called "historical sketches" quote from it as though it were fact. Mary Mornton emerges in several later versions of Lafitte's history as the great love of his life. As a matter of fact, Mary did not exist except in this now-forgotten romance.

Other fictional accounts followed, reaching their climax in 1836 when the Reverend Mr. Joseph H. H. Ingraham, that once-popular but now forgotten novelist of Maine and Mississippi, published his novel called "The Pirate of the Gulf, Lafitte." This peaceful teacher and clergyman had already changed Captain Kidd beyond recognition in a romantic novel, and, having a taste for pirates, he then turned his abundant energies upon Jean Lafitte. Here we have the handsome youth—the black sheep of a fine old family—who murders his brother in a moment of vexation, and leaves home for adventure on the briny deep. He becomes a pirate of the most san-

Lafitte the Pirate

guinary kind, and takes up his position upon an "impregnable rock" at Barataria. The novel is full of the best Victorian touches: ruined monasteries, crumbling castles of olden times (rather reminiscent of Sir Walter Scott, and surely unlike anything that existed in Louisiana at that time) where marble stairs led down to "still lagoons," and strong men fought duels with rapiers while frail females swooned. And again our hero is redeemed by the nobility of pure womanhood. Mary Mornton appears again, with her name changed to another which I have now forgotten; but it is our same lady, slightly altered, and still conforming to pattern.

In subsequent "histories" of Lafitte, we now find him as the black sheep of a noble family. Sometimes he has changed his name, and "his real title will never be known."

I mention the Reverend Mr. Ingraham's novel because the author's fanciful conception of the pirate is responsible for so much nonsense written afterwards as history. There is considerable correspondence of the novelist's published in DeBow's Review in 1852, when a controversy raged concerning Lafitte; and, at that time, Mr. Ingraham wrote to say that he had taken his material from the Reverend Mr. Timothy Flint's history. But if we are curious enough to investigate Mr. Flint's yellowing pages, we find only a few scant paragraphs concerning the buccaneer at the Battle of New Orleans. Mr. Ingraham's correspondents taxed him with this, during the controversy, and his last letter is a masterpiece of

The Legendary Lafitte

poesy in which he quotes the Byron couplet already mentioned, and ends by saying:

"I found in my researches, twenty years ago, romantic legends so interwoven with facts that it was extremely difficult to separate the historical from the traditional. I am very sure that the same cause will make it impossible to arrive at the truth of his life. His only biographer at last must be the romancer."

This, in a sense, is true; but one can scarcely help deploring the fact that some of those earlier writers did not make the effort, while documents, records and papers were still at hand, and while many living men remembered Lafitte. This, however, appears to be too much to ask. The writers seem to prefer to invent their "documents" and arrange things to suit themselves. The case of George A. Pierce's "Life and Times of Jean Lafitte" is a shining example.

Fifteen years after the publication of Ingraham's romance, there was printed in DeBow's Review, for October 1851, a biographical sketch of Lafitte purporting to have been written by one Mr. George A. Pierce of Louisiana. Whether this article was concocted in good faith, or whether it was a deliberate literary hoax, with the editor of the review either a party or a victim in this perversion of history, I cannot say. In the storm of denials and accusations which followed—for many men then living had known Lafitte—the editor made haste to state that Mr. Pierce had died suddenly and could not defend

Lafitte the Pirate

himself or his statements. Mr. Pierce's "true account" of Lafitte, which he said was based upon documents and statements made by men who had been members of the Baratarian establishment, included every yarn and ridiculous extravaganza that helped to make the mythical pirate. It is interesting in that there is hardly one true thing in it: even the dates are almost uniformly wrong in all incidents which can be proved at this late date by court records and newspaper files. But the composition is magnificent for its adjectives, and for its gore.

According to the DeBow version, Jean Lafitte was born in St. Malo, France, in 1781. From early boyhood he lived but to sail the ocean blue. Before he reached his manhood he had made several voyages to seaports in Europe and Africa. In 1802 he shipped as first mate of a French East Indiaman bound for Madras. Off the cape of Good Hope, the ship was nearly wrecked in a gale, and a fire broke out in the hold, damaging the vessel so that the captain put in to the Mauritius. Lafitte quarreled with the captain, and as his "haughty spirit never brooked control" he abandoned the ship in disgust. From that moment began his illegal connection with the ocean. "His restless spirit had been inflamed by the romantic exploits of the hardy buccaneers of the time, whose names and deeds had resounded over every land and sea; and he resolved to imitate, if not surpass, their most brilliant actions, and leave a fame to the future that would not soon be forgotten."

The Legendary Lafitte

Our boy pirate now climbs the ladder of buccaneering fame with the agility of a monkey. French privateers were fitting out at Fort St. Louis to attack British commerce. Lafitte "accepted" the command of a beautiful, fast-sailing vessel of 200 tons, with two guns and twenty-six men, and spared no pains to make her the pride of the sea. He sailed forth and attacked indiscriminately weaker vessels under any flag that he happened to meet. He accumulated vast sums of gold and silver, enriching himself and his crew, only to "cast them away in profligacy and liberality."

Then he went into the slave trade. While taking a cargo of negroes from the Seychelles to the Mauritius, he was chased as far north as the equator by an English man-of-war. Escaping, but being without provisions, he put his helm about, with the energy and boldness characteristic of him, and made for the Bay of Bengal. He captured an armed English schooner superior to his own and put his crew aboard after killing off the former crew. Before long, sailing gaily along in his new vessel, he fell in with the *Pagoda,* an English East Indiaman, carrying 26 guns and 150 men. Lafitte so maneuvered as to make the Englishmen believe he was a Ganges pilot. As soon as possible he boarded the *Pagoda* with his nineteen men, all with cutlasses in hand. His crew defeated the 150 Englishmen, putting the sword to all who resisted them. Again he transferred his command to the captured ship and sailed back to the Mauritius, where he sold his

Lafitte the Pirate

prizes and bought for a new venture, a strong, well-built ship, named *La Confiance* and manned by 250 bold pirates.

His second cruise in *La Confiance* began in 1807. According to his biographer, this cruise was marked with the same desperation, valor, skilful navigation and pecuniary success as had distinguished his previous efforts. He soon fell in with the *Queen,* a large British vessel, pierced for forty guns and carrying 400 men. Lafitte sighted her off "Sand's Head," somewhere off the coast of British India:

The *Queen* moved majestic on her way as if in defiance of his inferior force. Lafitte resolved to take her. He addressed a powerful speech to his men, exciting their wildest imaginations. Every man waved his hat and hand and cried aloud for action. The *Queen* bore down on him and gave him a tremendous broadside, which, owing to the height, did but little execution. Before the action, Lafitte had ordered his men to lie down on the decks. The British captain believed that all were killed or wounded, and came alongside to grapple and board. At this moment Lafitte gave a whistle, and in an instant the deck bristled with armed men. While the smoke prevailed he ordered his men into the tops and yards, whence they poured an incessant fire of shells, bombs, and grenades into the forecastle of the Indiaman, producing such slaughter among the crew that they were forced to withdraw. At this crisis, Lafitte beat to arms, and placing a favorite at the head of forty men, with pistols in their hands and daggers in their clenched teeth, ordered them to board. Lafitte followed at

The Legendary Lafitte

the head of a second division of boarders. He himself engaged the captain of the *Queen,* and after a severe conflict, slew him. Still the English crew fought bravely. Lafitte pointed at them a swivel gun, charged with grape and canister; and seeing that extermination was inevitable, they surrendered. The vessel was plundered, and a large amount of gold and silver was divided among *La Confiance's* crew.

And if that isn't a pretty bit of invention, I'd like to see one. However, Mr. Pierce is only warming up. He can do better without half trying.

The capture of the *Queen* and many similar exploits, with never a failure, produced such a panic in British commerce that no ships went to India afterwards without a strong convoy. So Lafitte decided to sail home. However, in the Gulf of Guinea, he captured two valuable prizes laden with palm-oil, ivory, gold and other nice things. At St. Malo he sold *La Confiance* and his prizes with their cargoes, and "trod once more his native soil, opulent and renowned, where, ten years previous, he was hardly known."

Lafitte's next step, according to this biography by Mr. Pierce, was toward the western continent. He was not long inactive. "His restless spirit, like a caged eagle, longed once more for his native element, the breeze, the battle, and the storm." The delightful and wealthy pirate now turned his attention from the East Indies to the West Indies. Illustrious success accompanied him everywhere. In a brigantine with 20 guns and 150 men, with

Lafitte the Pirate

the French Island of Guadeloupe as headquarters, he swooped down once more on British commerce. Later he transferred his headquarters to Barataria, sailing under the flag of Carthagena. And, still according to Pierce, he now acquired the title of "The Terror of the Gulf."

The trouble with this part of the story is that we have now come to the part of Lafitte's life where many things are definitely known; and it is quite certain that he was no terror when he operated his blacksmith shop in New Orleans in 1809; nor did he possess any such reputation until after he was driven out of Galveston in 1821.

Mr. Pierce then goes on to describe the affairs of Barataria, and tells the story of the reward which Claiborne offered for the corsair's *head*, and of how the pirate promptly offered *fifteen thousand dollars* for Claiborne's head. He also gives an interesting version of how Lafitte bought off the custom officials:

The Governor sent an expedition to approach Lafitte's fortifications, to capture the pirates and bring them to New Orleans for trial. The expedition was headed by a man who had served under Lafitte and knew the ground. Lafitte permitted the expedition to approach, and then at his signal, the entire party of invaders was surrounded and captured before it could strike a blow. It was on this occasion that Lafitte showed that characteristic nobleness and generosity of character which glistens like a jewel in the darkness of a thousand crimes. Instead of executing the men who had come to take away his life and all that was dear to him, he loaded them

280

with costly presents and suffered them to return unmolested
to New Orleans.

When Pierce reaches the part concerning the Battle
of New Orleans, he cannot restrain himself. Here Lafitte
"raved like a lion amid his fury, cutting down two British
officers in command with his own arm." This is news indeed.

I will pass over this writer's version of the establishment at Galveston, and give instead the truly magnificent
description of Lafitte's last fight. According to Pierce,
our hero now sailed forth "like an evil spirit to war
against the world." A British sloop of war chased him
and overhauled him in the Gulf (year not stated) and a
dreadful struggle ensued:

Above the storm of battle, Lafitte's stern voice was heard,
and his red arm, streaming with gore and grasping a shat-
tered blade, was seen in the darkest of the conflict. The blood
now ran in torrents from the scuppers and dyed the waters
with a crimson stain. At length Lafitte fell, wounded des-
perately in two places. A ball had broken the bone of his right
leg; a cutlass had penetrated his stomach. The commander
of the boarders was stretched senseless on the deck close by
Lafitte, and the desperate pirate, beholding his victim within
his grasp, raised himself to slay the unconscious man. Lafitte
threw his clotted locks aside, drew his hand across his brow
to clear his sight of blood and mist, and raised the glittering
blade above the heart of the dying man. But his brain was
dizzy and his aim unsure, and the dagger descending, pierced

Lafitte the Pirate

the thigh of his powerless foe, and Lafitte fell back exhausted on the deck. Again reviving, with the convulsive grasp of death, he essayed again to plunge the dagger in the heart of his foe, but as he held it over his breast, the effort to strike broke the slender ligament of life, and Jean Lafitte was no more!

A pretty death indeed for our "Terror of the Gulf" but as purely imaginary as the rest of Mr. Pierce's narrative.

The article in DeBow's Review brought forth literary hoots and catcalls, and a vast amount of amazing information. The writers nearly all stated that they had known Lafitte, and had heard the truth from his own lips. Here are some of the things they wrote:

He was not born at St. Malo, but in a little village on the Garonne; not on the Garonne, but at Marseilles; not at Marseilles but Bayonne; not at Bayonne, but at Bordeaux. Lafitte was not a sailor at all, but a captain in Napoleon's army; not in Napoleon's army, but a fencing-master, both in France and in Louisiana; not a fencing-master, but a hapless young man who had gone to sea, and had been captured by cruel Spaniards, imprisoned at Havana for years, and had vowed vengeance on Spain; his whole life was but a blood vendetta against Spain, and that he never attacked any but Spanish vessels. Still another wrote that he was a French sailor who had been so badly treated by the English that he vowed vengeance and turned pirate with the one idea of destroying Eng-

The Legendary Lafitte

lish shipping; that his family and friends tried to turn his mind to nobler things, but that he cursed them crying: "If I do go to hell, I will drag plenty of Englishmen with me." The same witness declares that Lafitte told him that he had a wife who was killed by the Spaniards. Another tells a similar story, only the English are blamed for the young lady's untimely death. Still another witness wrote that Lafitte had married and had returned to France; that he was not dead at all but living in domestic bliss with his dear little children climbing upon his knee.

All of which was very interesting, but did not clarify the history of the pirate to any great extent. It does bring out one interesting thing however: Lafitte told scores of conflicting stories concerning himself. This is not altogether surprising, when one considers that his career was built up largely upon duplicity and double-dealing; and it appears that, toward the last, he lied for the sheer joy of lying, long after the time when such lies could have been of benefit to him. Many of the wild tales concerning him seem to have come from the man himself. This is probably the key to his mysteriousness. He transformed himself into a legend while he was still alive.

The historians of Louisiana are frank in saying that they know nothing of the boyhood of Jean Lafitte; but Yoakum of Texas, whose history was published in 1856, says that Lafitte was a runaway from France and a sailor on the British frigate *Fox*. He deserted, lived for a time with a French family in Deptford, took passage to South

Lafitte the Pirate

America, lived in Carthagena and afterwards at Santa Martha, became a privateer when the struggle for independence began in New Grenada, visited several ports in the United States, including Charleston, where he killed a rival in a love affair, and finally found his way to New Orleans and Barataria. It is amusing to compare this account with that of the writer in De Bow's Review; and the fact that Mr. Yoakum's history of Texas was written five years later than Mr. Pierce's would indicate that he was familiar with Pierce's story and did not believe it. Where Mr. Yoakum got his material, I do not know, but his standing as a historian is unquestioned; and it is certain that he did not include his story of Lafitte's early life without some sort of investigation.

But Pierce's "biography" caused trouble enough for those who were to write of Lafitte afterwards; in fully fifty subsequent articles, both in magazines and newspapers, Pierce's wild tales are given as truth; this further complicates the research-worker's task. It is a remarkable thing, but the more incredible a story is, the more easily the unthinking seem to believe it. Pierce's tale, despite the storm of denials which followed, and despite the fact that the editor of DeBow's Review ultimately disclaimed all responsibility for it, has been swallowed whole by many men who should have known better. It has even been reprinted in reputable historical magazines.

Of the scores of lesser writers who have added additional impossible "facts" concerning Lafitte, it is

The Legendary Lafitte

unnecessary to speak. Nor is it necessary to mention the dozen or more novels of which Jean Lafitte is the hero, or villain, as the case may be. Novelists are privileged to do what they please with fictional characters.

The legends in Louisiana concerning the pirate, and particularly concerning his buried treasures, are legion. Most of them do not stand investigation; many others are so unimportant that they are hardly worth considering. The legends at Grande Terre and Grande Isle are but fragments. Most of the descendants of the pirates will not admit that fact; they seem to feel that a punishment of some sort may fall upon them from the Federal Government, even at this late date. Both islands have been swept by tropical hurricanes, and the papers and souvenirs of the families have been destroyed.

In the bibliography which follows, I have listed the histories, magazine articles, letters and documents which I have examined in compiling this book. This is, of course, only a portion of what has been written about Jean Lafitte. The novels, plays and other fictional stories are not listed; but there are scores of them.

In the material concerning Lafitte I have found many repetitions; and although a great mass of printed matter was read, the facts remain meager enough. It is extremely difficult to differentiate between fact and fiction, but I have made every effort to do so. No story has been used without examination; and if the material is traditional, I have indicated it as such.

Lafitte the Pirate

Before leaving the legendary Lafitte, one more story must be considered. It was published in the New Orleans "States" in 1928, on August 19th, August 26th, September 2nd and September 9th. The articles were written by Meigs O. Frost, and were a series of interviews with Dr. Louis Julian Genella of New Orleans. Let me quote the introductory paragraphs:

Some twenty-five miles south of New Orleans is an ancient burial ground. It lies on the high point of land that juts out . . . where the Bayou of the Geese flows into Big Barataria Bayou. There, in a tangle of wild rose bushes and tall grass, stands an iron cross. . . . That cross marks an old, sunken grave. Two other ancient graves are nearby.

Now, for the first time, the story is given to the world that in one of those graves sleep the remains of Napoleon Bonaparte. That in another of those graves sleeps John Paul Jones, the great American admiral of the Revolution. And that in the third grave, beneath the iron cross, rests the man history knows as Jean Lafitte, the buccaneer of Barataria!

More than that. The considered statement is also made that Jean Lafitte, the dashing sea-raider who looted the ships of the Spanish Main, was the *cousin of Napoleon Bonaparte;* the *nephew of John Paul Jones.* That Lafitte really did rescue Napoleon from Saint Helena, leaving a substitute, almost a "double" of the conqueror in his place. That Jean Lafitte fought side by side with John Paul Jones in the immortal battle between the British frigate *Serapis* and America's little *Bonhomme Richard,* winning the battle with the first breech-loading gun in naval history, his own invention.

That it was the same type of gun, planted on the west bank

286

The Legendary Lafitte

of the Mississippi, with which Jean Lafitte hurled destruction into the British ranks when the Baratarian buccaneer fought side by side with General Andrew Jackson at the Battle of New Orleans, and won from President Madison a pardon for himself and all his men. That Jean Lafitte went to the little Breton village where John Paul Jones died after his service under the Empress Catherine of Russia, and brought the body of his uncle back to Barataria.

Furthermore, that alien bones rest in the tomb of the Hôtel des Invalides in Paris, which history gives as Napoleon's last resting place; and in the tomb at the United States Academy at Annapolis, where Admiral John Paul Jones is supposed to sleep. . . .

Fantastic statements. A story that upsets the ordered tale on the pages of history. The historians can fight it out. They have a man to fight. For that astounding story is not fatherless. It is made public after long years of study by Dr. Louis Julian Genella, M. D., of New Orleans.

An interview with Dr. Genella follows; an interview so long that it is continued in newspaper stories for four Sundays. He first tells of his life-long interest in Lafitte, then of finding "an ancient chest of faded documents, written in ink, stored away in the attic of a very distinguished New Orleans family. . . . The name of that family, I regret, cannot be made public. . . . They are lineal descendants of a man I give the fictitious name of Anarb de Seville. . . . He was a leader of Jean Lafitte's buccaneers. The man was Homeric. Gigantic in stature. Always wore gold earrings in his ears and his head was

Lafitte the Pirate

covered with a bright crimson silken handkerchief. . . ."

Dr. Genella then goes on to tell his story with gusto. Here is a mass of detail; long conversations are quoted. He tells that Jean Lafitte was the illegitimate son of "Jessica Corsica Bonaparte" and "William Paul" brother of John Paul (Jones); that Lafitte was born in Louisiana, but went early in life to France, where he soon became famous as "Jean of St. Malo." That Pierre Lafitte was only his foster-brother, and that Jean took his name. That Joseph Lafitte, another foster-brother, was secretary to Joseph Bonaparte. That there were other foster-brothers, Henri and Marc (or Antoine). . . . That on January 18, 1819, Jean Lafitte did actually reach St. Helena and rescue Napoleon, leaving an imposter in his place; but that Napoleon died at sea, off the coast of Yucatan. Dr. Genella says that Lafitte brought Napoleon's body to Louisiana and buried it beside Goose Bayou. The writer then goes on to tell of the invention of the breech-loading cannon, and of how Lafitte really won John Paul Jones's battle for him. Here again we have long, quoted conversations, and we learn somewhat to our surprise, that Lafitte wore on shipboard "a gold band about his head." A crown.

Another installment of Dr. Genella's story deals with Andrew Jackson at New Orleans, and there is a dialogue between Lafitte and Jackson, giving a word-for-word account of the bargain they struck pertaining to the pardon for the Baratarians, and there is an account of Lafitte's

The Legendary Lafitte

part in the Battle of New Orleans, all different from the familiar historic record.

The last chapter tells of the end of Jean Lafitte. He fought with a British ship in the Mexican Gulf, was wounded fatally, and before his death gave orders that he be buried on Goose Bayou beside his cousin Napoleon and his uncle Jones. And, concludes Dr. Genella, there he lies —or rather there all three of them lie—in unmarked graves. Above Lafitte's body there rises the iron cross. There is no name upon it.

Dr. Genella says that he cannot produce his proof now because the descendants of the man he calls Anarb de Seville do not wish to have their names linked with such disclosures. He cannot embarrass his friends.

The whole tale is so contrary to all known facts, that historians must demand sure proof before they can accept it. Nothing short of letters by Napoleon, written after he left St. Helena, would be acceptable; as the facts of Napoleon's life and death have been so carefully studied by so many men. The John Paul Jones story, too, needs documentary proof.

One cannot help hoping that Dr. Genella can prove his statements. For how interesting they are, and what a swashbuckling fellow Lafitte appears to be. But until such proof is produced, the writer of history must regard Dr. Genella's story as legend, rather than as fact.

Chapter XXXII

BURIED TREASURE

FOR more than a century men have searched for the buried treasure of the pirate Lafitte. The search has covered a thousand miles along the Mexican Gulf, and has included every bay, inlet and bayou from Key West to the mouth of the Rio Grande. Through all these years strange tales of hidden gold and jewels have been repeated, and the treasure has grown with each year that has passed.

Florida, Alabama, Mississippi, Louisiana and Texas, all have their legends. Some have to do with golden bars buried in the sand of a beach, or beneath a spreading tree; others tell of treasure-laden vessels which went to the bottom in storms; still others deal with scuttled ships, which rest now on the ocean's bed—or in bayou or bay

Buried Treasure

—where, locked away in iron chests, fabulous gems and doubloons without number await discovery.

The fact that numerous small sums have been found at long intervals—and at widely scattered points—has kept the legend alive; and there are always men, in each generation, who search. It would be easy to fill a volume with the fantastic tales of these treasure seekers. But a few examples must suffice.

In 1851, a sum of money was found on Caillou Island. The newspaper accounts are meager, but "it is rumored that twenty thousand dollars in Spanish doubloons were found." A later account in the same newspaper, put the sum at two thousand dollars.

But this find on Caillou started a search that was to continue for many years. The newspapers of that period tell of many expeditions setting sail; but I have been unable to find one story of a triumphant return.

The Gulf coast, it must be remembered, was for nearly a century Spanish territory; and the Spanish are renowned for hiding things away. There is an old saying, in the Gulf country, that a secretive person is "like a Spanish cat." For Spanish cats, you understand, buried trinkets as dogs bury bones—an assertion which you may take with a grain of salt, if you wish. But most of the discovered treasures were hidden in Spanish times.

Mississippi and Louisiana planters entombed their valuables during the Civil War, when these states were overrun with Federal troops. Some of the men who did

Lafitte the Pirate

so died in the Confederate army and their possessions remained in the earth. Others buried jewels and silver, left their homes and never returned. There are stories of people who "forgot" where things were placed, and their grandchildren are still hunting for them. Not very long ago, in making a hole for a gate post, a plantation family found more than a hundred bottles of fine old whiskey.

But every discovery, no matter how trivial, gives new faith to those who find it difficult to believe history, but easy to believe legend.

There was that strange man Newell—a printer of New Orleans—who searched for a lifetime for Lafitte's treasure. J. Frank Dobie, writing in the Yale Review in 1928, tells of that long search. Newell himself has become a legend now, but Mr. Dobie looked up the facts, and found them fantastic enough. In 1851, or thereabouts, Newell's father befriended an old seafaring man, who, in return for his kindness, gave the elder Newell a map showing where Lafitte had hidden his doubloons. The father died, but the son devoted his life to a search for the gold. It became his only interest. He had little money, so he worked at his trade until he made enough to fit out an expedition. But—and there is always a "but" in these stories—"the winds and tides were so constantly shifting these islands that he could never be sure which one his chart called for." Half a dozen times he returned to his work, saved and left again for a fresh start. He kept up his search for twenty years, but he never lost

Buried Treasure

hope. He was drowned at last when a tropical storm upset his boat.

Mr. Dobie gives five or more similar stories. Most of them end in frustration, occasionally in death.

But one story which he overlooked—and no wonder, as there are hundreds of them—was the crime of Dr. Deschamps, which created such a sensation in New Orleans in the eighteen eighties.

Deschamps was a dentist, and, it is said, a good one. He practised in New Orleans for a time, then became an itinerant practitioner, traveling through that rich territory which lay along Bayou Lafourche, where he attended the families of plantation owners. He was a pioneer in "painless" dentistry, using chloroform and hypnotism to quiet pain. In one of his rambles among the islands of the coast, once the hiding place of the buccaneers, he discovered some old coins and trinkets buried in the sand. From that moment he was a changed man; his imagination was inflamed with the idea of locating fabulous riches.

He had no faith in divining-rods, but he was sure that his powers as a hypnotist would serve him well. But he must find a suitable "subject."

Filled with this idea, he returned to New Orleans, and there become acquainted with the father of the girl who was to become his pitiful victim. The father, trusting the doctor, allowed the young girl—she was not yet sixteen—to spend long hours in the doctor's house. The dentist

Lafitte the Pirate

lived in an old Spanish residence at 714 Saint Peter Street, a house of barred doors and high walls, where it was possible to insure privacy. Under his training, the girl was frequently put to sleep. . . .

Soon, he made a secret expedition to the islands on the Gulf Coast, bringing the girl with him. At his subsequent trial, he told of a long night spent in the dark woods, where the girl, sleeping yet animate, wandered from place to place, trying to obey his commands. He believed that she would eventually point out the spot where the treasure lay.

Her failure to do so infuriated the half-crazed man; and, there in the dark woods, he beat and tortured the half-conscious girl. At his subsequent trial, it was brought out that he had used her for another purpose, as well.

He brought her back to New Orleans, believing now that she was somehow resisting him; and in the house on Saint Peter Street, he began to try experiments in order to bring her more completely into his power.

Her father suspected nothing; he was so full of trust that he allowed a younger daughter to go sometimes to the doctor's house. Finding that the older girl did not respond quickly enough to his hypnotic powers, Dr. Deschamps was now forced to give her chloroform in order to put her to sleep. One day, as the smaller girl watched, he gave the older sister too much of the drug. She died.

The doctor was overcome with horror, he cried and

Buried Treasure

became hysterical—as well he might. When the body was being prepared for burial it was found to be covered with bruises and scars, some not yet healed. The coroner made another discovery, and Dr. Deschamps was charged with murder and another crime.

He was found guilty on both counts, and sentenced to hang. He was a difficult prisoner, and quarreled with every one, including his own lawyers. After his conviction, he tried to bribe the jailor to let him escape, promising to divide Lafitte's treasure with him—as soon as he found it. This attempt failing, he went, cursing and railing against fate, to the scaffold.

In 1915, Henry Boudreaux, an Acadian of Abbeville, Louisiana, tried hypnotism in an attempt to locate the treasure. There was much excitement in the locality, as he made these attempts, using a little negro boy as a "subject." However, no fatalities resulted this time, and Boudreaux actually found an old silver platter and some other things at a spot pointed out. As the news spread, hundreds joined in the search, using divining-rods and other devices. But nothing more was turned up.

In 1925 a newspaper despatch to the Times Picayune, from Abbeville, tells of another epidemic of treasure-hunting, in which trees were uprooted with dynamite on Pecan Island. "Treasure hunting fever," the despatch concludes "has not been at so high a pitch since Henry

Lafitte the Pirate

Boudreaux and the hypnotized negro boy found the silver platter and the Dutch oven."

At that time, a vast treasure was reported found at Pecan Island; and as this was Lafitte territory, the treasure was, of course, Lafitte's treasure. Hundreds waited for two men—Theodore Veasey and Jim Morgan—to emerge from the swamp; but they emerged, according to the newspaper account, empty handed.

Here is the most recent newspaper notice that I have seen:

Bunkie, Louisiana, March 4th (1930). The proverbial end-of-the-rainbow story came true yesterday for Forest Normand, Avoyelles Parish farmer, when he plowed up a pot of silver coins on his farm near here. While plowing, he noticed a few coins turned up, and upon closer investigation, unearthed an old iron pot, rusty with age, containing more than three thousand pieces of Spanish silver, coins dated from 1763 to 1805. Included in the find, was an American silver dollar bearing the date 1804 with the likeness of George Washington thereon.

This dispatch was printed on the first page of every newspaper in the Gulf Coast region that day, and everywhere men read it and said: "Lafitte." For any treasure is Lafitte's treasure, so strong is the legend of the buccaneer.

Shortly after the finding of the pot of coins, these

296

Buried Treasure

two notices appeared in the Times-Picayune and ran for some time in the classified column:

At this moment, as you read this, men are digging for that lost gold; men have searched for a century, and they will continue to search. For legend persists when history is forgotten.

It seems improbable that Jean Lafitte left any great sum buried on the coast of the Gulf of Mexico; for in the latter part of his career, as we have seen, he was far from affluent. It is possible, of course, that in those

297

Lafitte the Pirate

earlier, gaudier and more prosperous times he buried
chests filled with golden doubloons and Pieces of Eight;
but if so, it is more than likely that he dug them up again.

BIBLIOGRAPHY

Gayarré, Charles, "History of Louisiana," 1866.
Latour's "Historical Memoir of Louisiana."
Fortier, Alceé, "History of Louisiana."
King, Grace, "New Orleans, The Place and The People," 1902.
King and Ficklen's "History of Louisiana."
Walker, Alexander, "Jackson and New Orleans," 1855.
Arthur, Stanley Clisby, "The Battle of New Orleans," 1915.
Nolte, Vincent, "Fifty Years in Both Hemispheres," 1854.
Cable, George W., "The Creoles of Louisiana," 1901.
"Guide to New Orleans," 1885.
Castellanos, Henri, "New Orleans, As it Was," 1905.
Yoakum's "History of Texas," 1856.
Scrapbooks of newspaper clippings compiled by Mrs. Cammie Henry of Melrose Plantation.
Documents, letters and papers lent by Mr. Henry Lanause of New Orleans.
Documents and miniature lent by James B. Pelletier of New Orleans.
Letters of Mrs. Vincent Perrault, of Natchez, Mississippi.
Letters now in the collection of E. A. Parsons, president of the Louisiana Historical Society.
Papers lent by G. William Nott of New Orleans.
Papers lent by Dr. Theodore Engelbach of Grande Isle.

Lafitte the Pirate

Files of the New Orleans Delta, Le Courier de la Louisiane, the New Orleans Advertiser, the New Orleans Gazette, the Times-Picayune, the Item, and the Daily States.
Papers and documents at the Cabildo, New Orleans.

(From this point, to the end of the bibliography, the books, magazine and newspaper articles, documents and letters mentioned will be found in the Rosenberg Library at Galveston. Texas.)

Niles Weekly Register—Nov. 5, 1814; Feb. 11, 1815; Feb. 5, 1820; Sept. 30, 1820; Jan 20, 1821; Dec. 22, 1821.
United States Magazine and Democratic Review, July 1839, "Cruise of the Enterprize; a day with Lafitte."
Foote, H. S., "Texas and the Texans," 1841.
Kennedy, William, "Texas," 1841.
Frost, John, "Pictorial Life of Andrew Jackson," 1847
DeBow's Review—Sept. 1851, "Life and Times of Lafitte," Pierce; Feb. 1852, "Lafitte," editorial; July 1852, "History of Lafitte," editorial; Aug. 1852, "Lafitte," W. H. K.; Oct. 1852, "Lafitte," Prof. Ingraham's letter; Dec. 1853, "Early Life in the Southwest"; Aug. 1853, "Lafitte the Pirate"; Sept. 1857, "Lafitte the Pirate."
Living Age—Mar. 6, 1852, "Life of Jean Lafitte."
Byron, Lord, Poetical Works (1857), "The Corsair." Footnotes of special value.
Galveston City Directory, 1859–60: article entitled "Early History of Galveston," Col. J. S. Thrasher.
Galveston City Directory, 1870: article entitled "Historic sketch."
Baker, D. W. C., comp. "Texas Scrap-Book," 1875.
Thrall, Homer S., "Pictorial History of Texas," 1879.

Bibliography

Magazines of American History—10: 284–298, 389–396, Oct. 1883: article entitled "Historical Sketch of Pierre and Jean Lafitte," Charles Gayarré.

Century Magazine—25: 859–867, April 1883: article entitled "The Pirates of Barataria," G. W. Cable.

Morrison, Andrew, "Industries of Galveston," 1887.

Atlantic Monthly—91: 806–814, June 1903: "Barataria: the Ruins of a Pirate Kingdom," Leonidas Hubbard, Jr.

Pennybacker, Mrs. A. J. H., "New History of Texas for Schools," 1888.

Bancroft, H. H., "History of the North Mexican States and Texas," 1889.

Morrison, Andrew, "The Port of Galveston," 1890.

Brown, John Henry, "History of Texas," 1892.

Wooten, D. G., "Comprehensive History of Texas, 1685–1897," 1898.

Wooten, D. G., "Complete History of Texas," 1899.

Ousley, Clarence, "Galveston in 1900": chapter entitled "History of Galveston."

Garrison, G. P., "Texas, a Contest of Civilizations," 1903.

"Outlines of the Transcendent Physical Advantages of Bolivar," 1874.

Texas State Historical Association Quarterly—6: 146–149, Oct. 1902, "The African Slave Trade in Texas," Eugene C. Barker; 6: 252, Jan. 1903, "Reminiscences of Early Texans," J. H. Kuykendall.

Bolton, Herbert and Barker, Eugene, "With the Makers of Texas."

Phelps, Albert, "Louisiana," 1905: chapter entitled "The War of 1812 and the Battle of New Orleans."

Elite Magazine—1: 13–15, Feb. 1907: article entitled "Lafitte, the Lord of Campeachy," E. C. Littlejohn.

Lafitte the Pirate

Gulf Coast Magazine—4: 7–23, Jan. 1909: article entitled "True story of Jean Lafitte," Victor Jean Lavalette.

Outing Magazine—58: 242–248, May 1911: article entitled "Lafitte, the last of the Buccaneers," John R. Spears.

Harper's Magazine—124: 80–91, Dec. 1911: article entitled "In the Haunts of Jean Lafitte," Frank E. Schoonover.

Munsey Magazine—28: 120–123, Oct. 1902, "True Story of Lafitte," J. R. Spears.

Pan American Magazine—16: 24–31, Sept. 1913, "Lafitte the Pirate Hero of Barataria and Galveston," A. J. Himel.

Tangent—3: 9–16, Jan. 1913: "If Lafitte Came Back," R. D. Frazier.

Powell, E. A., "Gentlemen Rovers," 1913: chapter entitled "Pirate Who Turned Patriot."

Stockton, Frank R., "Buccaneers and Pirates of Our Coasts," 1915: chapter entitled "The Pirate of the Gulf."

"Pirates' Own Book," 1924: chapter entitled "Life of Lafitte."

The Southwest Miller: p. 695, Feb. 14, 1923, "Galveston, the City and Port," I. D. McMaster.

Wortham, Louis J., "History of Texas," 1924: chapter entitled "Two decades of Friction."

American Mercury—7: 214–219, Feb. 1926: article entitled "Portrait of a Pirate," Walter B. Lister.

Rowland, Mrs. Dunbar, "Andrew Jackson's Campaign Against the British," 1926: p. 227, 233–234, 286–288.

Galveston News: thirty-one articles by various writers on various phases of Lafitte's life and history, between the dates 1874–1928.

Stuart, Ben C.: five articles in the Galveston News between the dates, Mar. 3, 1907–May 21, 1911. Rosenberg Library has clipped these articles and pasted them in a book known as the "Stuart Scrapbook."

Bibliography

Dyer, Dr. J. O.: forty-four articles in the Galveston News between the dates, Mar. 21, 1920–April 20, 1924. Rosenberg Library has clipped these articles and pasted them in a book known as the "Dyer Scrapbook."

Stuart, Ben C.: four unpublished articles in manuscript form that mention Lafitte in connection with subject of article.

Original letter written by Jean Lafitte on Galveston Island, July 7, 1819, to General James Long who was then at Nacogdoches.

Original navigation order issued by the Lafitte Commune on Galveston Island, April 2, 1818, signed by Jao de la Porta.

Original notice, dated Camp of Campeche, Isle of St. Louis, 15 May 1818, signed by Jean Lafitte.

Coleman, W. H., comp. ". . . Historical Sketch Book and Guide to New Orleans," chapter entitled "Lafitte, the Pirate," 1845.

Adams, Henry, "History of the United States."

Encyclopedia Americana, vol. 16, p. 650.

Appleton's Cyclopedia of American Biography, vol. 3, pp. 590–591.

Appleton's New Practical Cyclopedia, vol. 3, p. 490.

Davis, M. E. M., "Under Six Flags," pp. 40–48.

McMaster, J. B., "History of the People of the United States," vol. 4, pp. 174–177.

Nelson's Loose-Leaf Encyclopaedia, vol. 7, p. 178.

New International Encyclopædia, vol. 13, pp. 461–462.

Parton, James, "Life of Andrew Jackson," vol. 1, pp. 580–590.

Chamberlin, J. E., "Ifs of History," 1907: chapter entitled "If the Pirate Jean Lafitte Had Joined the British at New Orleans."

Lafitte the Pirate

Rowland, Dunbar, ed. Official letter books of W. C. C. Claiborne, 1801–1816. (1917)

Verrill, A. H., "Boys' Book of Buccaneers," 1923.

Frontier Times—1: 24–26, May 1924, "Buried Treasure of Jean Lafitte."

Johnston, C. H. L., "Famous Privateersmen and Adventurers of the Sea," 1925: chapter entitled "Lafitte, Privateer, Pirate and Terror of the Gulf of Mexico (1780–1826)."

Louisiana Historical Quarterly—8: 341–368, July 1925: article entitled "Piracy in the Gulf of Mexico, 1816–1823," J. S. Kendall.

Frontier Times—3: 33–39, May 1926, "Vindication of Jean Lafitte."

Pan-American Magazine—13: 7–9: article entitled "Brave Tale of Texas."

Martin, F. X., "History of Louisiana," 1882.

Paine, R. D. "Fight for a Free Sea," Chronicles of America, 1920.

Stephenson, N. W., "Texas and the Mexican War," Chronicles of America, 1921.

Gosse, Philip, "Pirates' Who's Who," 1924.

Dallas News, Nov. 5, 1906.

Galveston Tribune: dates between Jan. 12, 1896 and Sept. 30, 1926.

Houston Chronicle: dates between Jan. 26, 1908 and Dec. 5, 1926.

New Orleans States: dates between Aug. 19, 1928 and Sept. 9, 1928.

New York Sun: June 25, 1893.

San Antonio Express: June 21, 1927.

Hutchison, J. R., "Reminiscences, Sketches and Addresses," 1874: chapter entitled "Galveston Island."

Bibliography

Scharnwober, W. A., "Facts about Galveston, Texas," 1899: chapter entitled "Galveston Island Early History."

Mississippi Historical Society. Publications: Centenary Series, v. 4., p. 112–113, 1921.

Yale Review: Autumn, 1928, p. 116–134, "Mystery of Lafitte's Treasure," J. Frank Dobie.

Southern Literary Messenger—2: 593, Aug. 1836: Review of Prof. Ingraham's "Lafitte: the Pirate of the Gulf."

Debates & proceedings in the Congress of the United States— 15th Congress, 2nd Session, Nov. 16, 1818—Mar. 3, 1819; comp. from authentic materials (1855) pp. 1948–1949.

DeBow's Review—13: 381, Oct. 1852. Article entitled "Early life in the Southwest—the Bowies."

Le Plongeon, A. D., "Here and There in Yucatan," 1886.

Louisiana Historical Quarterly—11: 434–444, July 1928: article entitled "Visit to Lafitte," Elliot Snow.

Stephens, J. L., "Incidents of Travel in Yucatan," 1843: 2v2, p. 358.

Stone & Webster Journal: Nov. 1928: article entitled "Jean Lafitte, the Buccaneer," H. M. Robinson.

Saxon, Lyle, "Father Mississippi," 1927.

Dill, M. G., "Footprints of Texas History," 1902.

Texas Monthly—4: 642–645, Dec. 1929: Martin, "Pirate of the Gulf."

Encyclopædia Britannica, 14th edition, vol. 13, p. 589.

LETTERS AND MANUSCRIPTS

Letter from James Brown, Senate Chamber, Oct. 1, 1814, to Hon. James Monroe, mentioning escape of (Pierre) Lafitte from jail.

Lafitte the Pirate

Letter from Edward Livingston, New Orleans, Oct. 24, 1814, to the President of the U. S. (James Madison), recommending a pardon for the Baratarians.

Letter from Jn. Lafitte, Washington, Dec. 27, 1815, to the President of the U. S.

Extract from a letter from James Long to Lafitte, June 24, 1819.

Letter from Jean Lafitte, Galveston, Texas, to James Long, Nacogdoches, Texas, Sept. 30, 1819.

Extract from a translation made by Mr. Stanley Faye, of a letter from John Lafitte, New Orleans, La., to Juan Manuel de Cagigal, Cuba, Dec. 11, 1819.

Letter from S. Rhoades Fisher, Houston, Texas, to Gen. Mirabeau B. Lamar, Feb. 26, 1838, concerning Lafitte.

Letter from S. Rhoades Fisher, Matagorda, Texas, to Gen. Lamar, Houston, Texas, May 1, 1838, concerning death of Lafitte.

Manuscript entitled "Information derived from James Campbell, June 10, 1855."

REFERENCES IN LAMAR PAPERS TO JEAN LAFITTE

No. 19.   Lafitte to Long, July 7, 1819. Aid to Long.
No. 24.   Lafitte to Long, September 30, 1819. Ibid.
No. 286.   Barataria and Lafitte, 1835 (?). Biography of Lamar.
No. 680.   S. R. Fisher to Lamar, February 26, 1838. The Death of Lafitte.
No. 719.   S. R. Fisher to Lamar, May 1, 1838. The Death of Lafitte.
No. 1611. Lafitte; Beal's search for the remnant of Long's expedition; Baron Bastrop. Sketch by Lamar, 1839.

Bibliography

No. 1612. Information from Col. S. M. Williams respecting Lafitte, 1839.

No. 2492. Information derived from James Campbell concerning his naval service, his privateering career with Rapp and with Lafitte, Lafitte's last days, Long. June 10, 1855.

No. 2800. History of the early attempt of foreigners to gain a foothold or to colonize in Texas; Nolan; John Brady; Bastrop; Richard R. Keene; Lafitte, etc. Sketch by Lamar.

No. 1614. Lafitte's duel with a South Carolinian; his establishment at Galveston. Sketch by Lamar.